SACRED BROTHERHOOD

How a Father and Son's Passion for Motorcycles Transformed the Legal Industry

Ari Levenbaum

Sacred Brotherhood

How a Father and Son's Passion for Motorcycles Transformed the Legal Industry

ISBN: 978-1-946203-90-8

Disclaimer

This publication is designed to provide accurate and authoritative information regarding the subject matter contained within. It should be understood that the author and publisher are not engaged in rendering legal, accounting, or other financial service through this medium. The author and publisher shall not be liable for your misuse of this material and shall have neither liability nor responsibility to anyone with respect to any loss or damage caused or alleged to be caused, directly or indirectly, by the information contained in this book. The author and/or publisher do not guarantee that anyone following these strategies, suggestions, tips, ideas, or techniques will become successful. If legal advice or other expert assistance is required, the services of a competent professional should be sought.

Expert Press

www.ExpertPress.net

Table of Contents

TESTIMONIALS/ENDORSEMENTS

"The only way to understand the motorcycle world and its culture is by living within it and participating. For 20 years, Ari, Warren, and their team at Law Tigers have done just that. As a motorcycle rider and a part of this tight-knit community for most of my life, I can instantly spot a fake or wannabe — and the Law Tigers are the real deal. They attend and often sponsor all of the major motorcycle events throughout the country. I have been in the legal world for the past 40 years, and I helped pioneer legal advertising in 1978, so I know lawyers, legal marketing, and motorcycles. The Law Tigers combine their understanding and passion for motorcycles, marketing, and the law in a unique way that's proven to generate large numbers of motorcycle accident cases for their members. Their commitment to work only with the best trial lawyers, those dedicated to helping injured riders, is evident in their roster of current elite member firms. The Law Tigers have established a reputation of trustworthiness, credibility, and integrity, making them the preferred choice for motorcycle riders and their families during what is often the most difficult time of their lives."

– Harlan Schillinger
Legal Marketing Expert
HarlanSchillinger.com

"If you are a lawyer who represents motorcycle riders, you are missing out if you do not become a member of Law Tigers! For almost 20 years, Law Tigers has stewarded a national network of law firms representing injured riders. Motorcycle riders are a unique and special group, and Law Tigers has created a unique and special family of lawyers to represent their interests!"

– Mark Lanier
Founder, The Lanier Law Firm

"For over 20 years, Law Tigers have been leaders in marketing to and representing injured motorcycle riders throughout the country. Under Ari and Warren's leadership, Law Tigers has become a household name within the riding community. I have always said it's important to niche down, and the Law Tigers program is a perfect example of that, especially when it comes to developing a motorcycle injury practice. Put simply, they're a well-established brand that delivers results."

– Michael Mogill
Founder & CEO of Crisp Video
Author of "The Game Changing Attorney"

INTRODUCTION

Law Tigers is a national network of independent motorcycle accident attorneys who are committed to protecting fellow riders. Riding is in our blood. We live and breathe this lifestyle every day and are proud to be a part of a unique culture. We are forever grateful for the friends we've made, our personal and professional success, and the vast experiences we've had from being an integral part of the motorcycle riding community. Whether you're an experienced rider or you're new to riding, the satisfaction of helping an injured rider in need and the motorcycle community at large is beyond compare.

We are proud to share that our members have firsthand experience assisting motorcycle accident victims and have provided thousands of injured riders and their families with individualized and experienced representation. We are with them every step of the way, or as we like to say, "We've got your back."

By being relational rather than transactional, we are committed to serving as a resource for the community. Our passion for riding, marketing acumen, and legal expertise has built Law Tigers into a nationally recognized brand that serves riders throughout the United States. Continuing to champion for the rights of mistreated riders, Law Tigers has cultivated countless partnerships within the motorcycle community, including working with and supporting thousands of motorcycle shops, events, and organizations.

Serving as a resource to the motorcycle community is the core of what we do. Not only are we here to provide legal support but also to be an integral part of the riding community. Our vision is to be part of and stand with the motorcycle community. Our mission is to support all aspects of the motorcycle community, including rider education, charity, safety initiatives, and advocating for injured riders.

LAW TIGERS®
MOTORCYCLE LAWYERS

Chapter

1

Go West, Young Man

To know and understand the essence of Law Tigers, you must first learn of its origins. In 2001, my father, Warren Levenbaum, founded Law Tigers. Because the program was his brainchild, I asked him to share how it all started.

His story follows:

Born in 1946, I was the first of what is known as the baby-boomer generation. One of five children, I came from very humble beginnings. I grew up in Boston in a working-class neighborhood and considered myself a street kid. To survive, you had to go out, work, and take care of yourself. At the age of 10, I was out hustling on the streets of Boston, trying to make a buck here and there and help out where I could. I had multiple jobs at a young age, which helped instill a sense of motivation and drive in me. As I matured, my tenacity would eventually lay the foundation for my future successes.

Growing up, I did pretty well in school. I was fortunate enough to get into the Boston Latin School — America's first high school — which dates back to the 1630s. To get in, you had to take an exam or qualify based on your grades. Kids from all of the working-class neighborhoods in Boston had the chance to apply. It gave poor kids an opportunity to get an excellent high school education before college. It was a classic public school in structure, and it followed a traditional format. Believe it or not, to graduate, you had to take four years of either Latin or Greek. I chose Latin.

I graduated at the top of my class and went on to Boston University to pursue a degree in economics. Back then, I couldn't afford to go to school. Loans were not as readily available as today, so I worked three or four jobs just to get through college. I didn't join a fraternity. I didn't socialize. I commuted every day from the Dorchester area of Boston to the university — two hours there and two hours back. I took the trolley, the train, and the bus.

When I graduated from Boston University, it was the height of the Vietnam War. I was fortunate and got into an Army Reserve Unit instead of being sent to Vietnam, so I took a year off after college and did time in the military. Once I was out of the Reserves, I went to Suffolk University Law School for three years and graduated in 1972.

At this point, I had to ask myself the question, "Where do I go from here?" I had been commuting four hours a day from the Dorchester section of Boston to downtown for 11 years, and I didn't want to do it anymore. So, I thought to myself: *Go west, young man*. Why not? I was broke, but now I had a law degree. I figured that if it didn't work out, I could always come back.

I left Boston with my wife, my 5-week-old son Ari, and $200 in my pocket. I knew that with the right attitude, I could make it work. I was motivated, and I was a hard worker. So, that's how I ended up in Arizona in 1972.

Since I was starting somewhere new, I had to remind myself that I didn't have any connections and had to build myself up. At that time, lawyers couldn't just take the bar exam; you had to wait a year to establish residency. That first year in Arizona, I paid my dues and worked multiple odd jobs to support my family.

At that time, we lived in an apartment in Phoenix. Fortunately, I passed the bar on the first try and quickly got a job as a prosecutor in Phoenix, Maricopa County, which was surprising because had I stayed in Boston, I would have needed to know somebody or had a connection to get that kind of position. It was so refreshing to be hired based on merit rather than on who you know or political patronage.

I worked as a prosecutor for three years, learning the ropes as a trial lawyer. During my career, I became a prestigious trial lawyer prosecutor and specialized in various categories of criminal offenses ranging from embezzlement to robbery to murder. I learned so much during these three years. Not only did I meet a lot of people, but I also gained the ability to navigate the city, both professionally and otherwise. After my stint, I decided to hang out my proverbial shingle, a term used for a lawyer going out on their own.

For a former criminal prosecutor, the most logical step was to become a criminal defense lawyer, which I did for several years. In addition, I represented police officers going through divorces. But after doing criminal work for about four years, I felt it was time for a change.

That's when I found my real niche — commercial law. As a result of my work ethic and street smarts, I built up a practice very rapidly. Within three years, I had hired an associate attorney and additional staff. In Phoenix, I had grown from nothing to something.

My practice kept growing, and I eventually took in a partner. At that time, we were a general practice law firm, which meant we focused on divorce cases, criminal work, personal injury, and small business transactions. The practice kept growing; after several years, I had a number of lawyers working for me, along with a staff of 20. I was building my practice while raising my family. Ari, my firstborn, was only 5 weeks old when we came to Arizona. After we moved, we had two more children, my two daughters.

All three of my children were raised here in Arizona, and we had a great family life. I was working hard and was able to grow my practice and give my children an excellent upbringing and education.

A decade later, my law practice was still growing. Most people would have started to take it easy and relax at that point. However, unlike most lawyers, I don't care for golf. I have what I consider a Triple-A personality. I can't stay put. How could I ever be still long enough to putt a golf ball? To relax, in addition to spending time traveling with my family, I would ride out to the desert on my motorcycle. That's where it all started. My trips to the desert on the weekends were the beginning of the Law Tigers program.

For a couple of years, I went out riding early on Saturday and Sunday mornings by myself. Springtime was my favorite time to ride. The Phoenix desert is beautiful at that time of year. You get out there, and it's just you and the road — a fully immersive experience in nature. And because I always rode on weekend mornings, I didn't have to deal with the traffic or worry about not being seen and having a potential collision.

After this became my routine for a couple of years, I rode to Cave Creek, about 25 miles outside of Phoenix. It was a weekend getaway for a lot of motorcycle riders. They would meet for breakfast and congregate there. On my ride, three motorcycle riders passed me going in the opposite direction and waved. I've had these kinds of interactions in the past, but on this particular day, something dawned on me. I realized that there was a camaraderie among riders. Those riders didn't know me, but they waved at me like I was a friend. Where else does that happen in America? The truth is, it doesn't.

It certainly doesn't happen in a subway in Boston. I've also never experienced it while driving an automobile. This interaction is unique. It's a form of bonding — the bond and camaraderie of motorcycle riders. I went home with a gut feeling, and I was inclined to do something with it. I began to study and contemplated where I could go with this concept. I went to the library to research sources about this particular market, the motorcycle riding community. Primarily, I studied commercial psychology to look at the effect of waving to a stranger and how to convert that experience into a business opportunity.

In the United States, the motorcycle population amounts to about 12 million riders. I discovered there were more than 100,000 motorcycle accidents in the country each year, a substantial number. These statistics led me to believe that the motorcycle community was a significantly underserved segment, and I wondered how I could capitalize on that. In studying this market, I looked into branding and licensing. Nobody was licensing legal programs back then. At this point, I had the big picture: I wanted to start the Law Tigers brand under my law firm in Phoenix.

It all started with a hunch, so I wanted to test it out first in Phoenix and see how it went. I had a feeling that this was going to be a great opportunity, and I figured, if it worked in Phoenix, it could work anywhere in the United States. I was going to do what has been done with businesses all over the country — license a business model. I was the first law firm in the United States to create a brand like Law Tigers.

Once I started the program in Phoenix, it grew faster than I could have imagined, and I knew that I was onto something even bigger and better than I could have conceived. During the first couple of years, the phone didn't stop ringing. As a business innovator, I studied the marketplace and was able to find a niche that hadn't existed previously. The brand name itself also did wonders. It was a deliberate branding technique. Not only did people like the name Law Tigers, but it was unique and easy to remember. The tiger is a stately and cunning animal, and that association made the brand even more successful. Additionally, I acquired the 1-800-Law-Tigers vanity phone number and companion website, lawtigers.com.

After three years, I expanded the Law Tigers program under my law firm from Phoenix to Tucson. After that, we went to California, then on to Utah and New Mexico. We used our firm's lawyers, licensed in those states, as the program continued to grow. I didn't want to practice law or have my firm practice law in the remaining 46 states, so I figured that the best approach was to scale and license the business opportunity and marketing model across the country, and that's what I did.

Initially, I started slowly. Of course, I encountered a couple of bumps and had to shift some aspects of the program. Ari, my son, was instrumental in the growth process. He took the model to the next level as we continued to grow across the country and expand the business model. Since then, it's been a remarkably successful journey.

To date, we are innovators in terms of representing the motorcycle riding community, an underserved segment of the American population, across the United States. One hundred thousand motorcycle accidents a year is a significant number. Where do riders go in their time of need? Before Law Tigers, no one was fulfilling these needs. Nobody was there who could relate to injured riders. We built our business on the basis that we're not only trial lawyers, but we're part of the riding community, too. We're riders who relate to our clients and serve their interests in the event of a motorcycle accident. We're not ambulance chasers going after seriously injured riders; we're giving back to the community.

Not only do we offer support in times of need, but we're there every day. In terms of our outreach efforts, we prioritize giving back to the motorcycle riding community across the country. While we are focused on instilling a sense of community through our outreach, we also want to ingrain our brand in riders' minds. In the states where we operate, our branding techniques have allowed us to become a household name within the motorcycle riding community.

Law Tigers aims to lead within the motorcycle community. Innovative and passionate, we are now in 33 states and 50 different markets. Law Tigers firms in each state operate within the framework of our unique business model. Our goal in the next two years or less is to complete this phase and sell out the rest of the country. We're almost there. I started out being the managing partner of my law firm and then, concurrently, the Managing Director of Law Tigers. I'm 74 years old, and I love what I do. I come into work every day — retirement is not in my vocabulary.

Chapter

2

My Story

I am so proud of my father and what he's accomplished. He continues to serve as an inspiration, a mentor, and guiding light in all that I do. Now that you've heard his story, let me tell you mine.

I remember the first house we lived in — a small, 1,200-square-foot home in Glendale, Arizona. Looking back, I remember spending a lot of time with my neighbors, Georgette and Mike. They were an older, retired couple who didn't have any kids. Mike took me under his wing and treated me like the son he never had. In fact, he was the one who taught me how to ride a bike and took off my training wheels when I was 4 years old. I suppose this was my first experience riding on two wheels! It was around this time that my dad left the Maricopa County's Prosecutors Office and decided to go work for himself.

Very soon after, things changed. Dad experienced early success, though not to the degree he has now, and it significantly improved our lifestyle. I attribute his success to hard work, passion, and a keen understanding of business and the law. My dad has always been entrepreneurial, and those years laid the groundwork for the business we have today. In the early years, we spent our social time on motorcycles. As a child, some of my fondest memories are of riding the Honda 70 ATC that I got when I was 8 years old.

I rode it every day in my free time. I would go down the street, on the golf course, and just about everywhere. My love of riding became stronger each year. As I got older, I ultimately wanted something bigger. I went from a Honda 70 ATC to a 200S ATC, and then finally, to the fastest three-wheeler of all time, a 250R. Since I was older, my dad would take me to the desert. We would ride to the desert in North Scottsdale or to the Yuma Sand Dunes, and motorcycles just became a part of our lifestyle and leisure. After we moved, I even got myself into a bit of trouble when I rode my three-wheeler behind my home on the Orange Tree Golf Course and onto the main road to get to undeveloped dirt lots in Scottsdale. I loved it! You could never keep me off motorcycles, and I've owned quite a few over the years. Currently, I own a Harley-Davidson Dyna Low Rider S, a Harley-Davidson Road Glide Special, a Kawasaki Ninja, a Can-Am UTV, and several dirt bikes.

Riding with Dad are some of my fondest childhood memories. I soon formed my love of motorcycles and dirt bikes. Growing up, I couldn't wait to be old enough to get my license. Along with my Honda XL 80, I also had a scooter I rode to work, school, and part-time jobs before I had my license. In high school, I worked at different times as a butcher's helper, a pizza delivery person, a table busser, and a Chinese buffet dishwasher to pay for my insurance.

While I was a slightly above-average student, I struggled academically and socially during the first two years of high school. I attended Chaparral High School in Scottsdale, Arizona. During my junior and senior years, I blossomed, making many friends and becoming part of the social crowd. While I was by no means an academic, I knew how to do well enough to maintain the grades necessary to get into a state university. I wasn't too concerned about getting into the best college, but I knew that postsecondary education was expected of me.

I soon went off to college, along with a bunch of my high school buddies. Instead of staying local and going to Arizona State, I decided to head to the University of Arizona to get the authentic college experience. Although many of my friends were also attending U of A, I was overwhelmed with the transition. I went from a relatively small, private grade school to a midsize high school to a large state university, a vastly different environment. While it was a challenge at first, I stuck it out and soon adjusted. Once I felt more comfortable, I began to enjoy the college experience, taking school more seriously and fully integrating into the environment. After I got involved, I experienced a well-rounded college experience, both academically and socially, which included involvement in various student honoraries, student government, a fraternity, and several campus clubs and organizations.

As I became immersed in the college experience, I believed I wanted to be a lawyer. I thought to myself: *My dad's a successful lawyer and loves what he does, so I might as well do the same.* I was in the prelaw fraternity and other organizations. While my educational track was law, I didn't do too well on the pre-LSAT and knew that my test scores wouldn't get me into many law schools. I decided to finish college, emphasizing my extra-curricular activities and awards, and hoped that I could get into some decent schools. After graduating, I took a year off, moved home, and started working. I took an LSAT class and started substitute teaching to pay for food, gas, and entertainment. Though the students ate me alive at first, I enjoyed the classroom experience, including the students' energy and enthusiasm. I taught a couple of days a week and studied for the LSAT, regularly taking practice tests. My performance improved, and I kept on studying, eventually scoring in the 95th percentile.

With that high score, my 3.7 GPA, and my other achievements, I figured I could get into some excellent schools. I applied to about 18 law schools and was accepted to most of them. I received scholarships as well and ultimately accepted an offer from the University of Southern California Law School with a partial scholarship. Unfortunately, I neglected to consider what it took to become a lawyer and, instead, focused more on following in my dad's footsteps rather than on the academic, intellectual, and other skills I needed.

Once accepted, I moved in with a friend from my University of Arizona years. I went to my first class and was immediately overwhelmed. I never fully understood the rigors of law school. In college, I studied and read, but law school was a whole different level. I was 22 years old and started to feel as if I wasn't there for the right reasons. Law school didn't interest me. I met with the dean, deferred my enrollment for a year, and decided to move back home and reevaluate my life.

I began to think that helping people in some other way would make me happy. I decided to reprioritize my life and goals. Realizing that money is not the only thing in life, I chose to pursue something that would fulfill me. I never thought that I wanted to be a teacher, but that's what I did. Eventually, I went back to school and got a degree in education and a master's in school administration. I worked as a substitute teacher while I earned my teaching certificate and eventually became a full-time teacher. I imagined that down the line, I'd pursue a role as a principal, but I enjoyed teaching, the kids liked me, and I was fulfilled.

While teaching was great, the money wasn't. Because there was no funding from the district, I paid for all my own supplies. To supplement my income and maintain my lifestyle, I always worked a second job. I did everything from working at a restaurant on the weekends and during the summers to selling mattresses. Like my dad, I developed a strong work ethic and did whatever it took to make ends meet.

About three years into my teaching career, my father came up with the idea for Law Tigers. I thought it was a little odd at first, so during that first year, I wasn't really involved with the program. Dad would practice law by day and do a few events during the weekends. Initially, he hired someone to help him out with event marketing, but after a year or so, he asked me to take this person's place. I remember him offering me $20 an hour to work motorcycle events and visit motorcycle shops.

In the beginning, I was reluctant because I already had the teaching job, but Dad convinced me to give it a shot, and I started working with him. At first, I attended some events and helped him hand out promotional materials. We would set up our little 13-foot trailer and tent at events, and I would visit shops on the weekend, evenings, and summers during the program's early stages. We would only do a handful of events a year, and we didn't have a consistent shop presence. I would go in and restock stands, hand out promotional items, and get to know people. After some time passed, our efforts really started to take off, and his law firm began to see an increase in case volume. I continued my part-time role with Law Tigers while teaching full-time for about four more years.

As Law Tigers continued to grow and expand out of state, Dad needed additional help, so he made me a generous offer to come work for him full time. It ended up being perfect timing as I had decided to end my teaching career. With that decision, everything changed.

Chapter
3

Law Tigers: The Early Years

During the early years of working full-time for Law Tigers, I performed dual roles. I was fulfilling a Marketing Manager role for my dad's firm while also functioning as the Marketing Director for other law firms that had licensed the program model. My job was to make things happen, ultimately generating motorcycle leads that resulted in cases. Over the years, our needs evolved, and I took on new roles and additional responsibilities to help grow business. Not only was I the first Marketing Manager to go around to shops and attend events, but I also had to train and oversee other Marketing Managers. Taking on so many different responsibilities and tasks helped me appreciate and understand the issues, obstacles, and wins associated with each role.

Early on, we sold a handful of markets. At that time, my dad was primarily responsible for the business development and selling of the program. Then, I would come in, launch it, and be responsible for management and oversight. At first, I had no idea what I was doing. Still, I did my best to get us into shops, develop relationships with clubs and organizations, schedule and attend events, and train and support the Marketing Managers. We experienced some failures, but measurably more successes in those early days. Back then, my primary goal was to fill any void, so I was planning national event participation, conducting market visits, and making sure that the Marketing Managers were visiting shops, attending events, and building our brand. While we didn't have the structure in place that we have today, I was proud of the work we were doing.

Considering that we started the program before the boom of the digital age, we had to rely on grassroots and traditional marketing to drive business. While filling a Marketing Director role, I was also buying media and overseeing a handful of markets. At that time, we had 13 Western markets in total — five of which were my father's. As we continued to learn about how best to market the program, I was motivated to transform and improve our operations with the help of dedicated team members into what it is today. We were able to see and address the program's inefficiencies and vulnerabilities. Not only was I looking at who we selected and how we supported the members, but I wanted to implement more support, direction, and oversight of the program.

What makes Law Tigers successful is our team of dedicated professionals, along with infrastructure, our ability to execute, and our willingness to continue to evolve and improve the systems, practices, and processes through teamwork and collaboration. Law Tigers continues to grow, and we're adding over a dozen new markets each year. When we felt that we had our program under control, we applied these same principles to our other members. Those with the patience, legal expertise, and financial means did very well and remain part of Law Tigers today. I'd like to recognize those early members — Tim, Michael, and Beth from Kelly Law Offices in Chicago; Tom and Janet from Metier Law Firm in Colorado; and Wes, Kyle, and David from Farrar & Ball in Houston — for their trust in us and long-term dedication to our program.

If we wanted to continue our growth, I knew that some things needed to change and evolve. About five years ago, I began instituting some of these changes. Until then, I had been an AAMIL (the Law Tigers licensing company) employee, not an owner. When things began to shift within my father's law firm, I had an opportunity to buy out my father's former silent partner in AAMIL, who was also his law partner. When that happened, I started to think about things a little differently because I now had some skin in the game as an owner. While I could see short-term gains through some new practices, I started thinking about how we could transform this business into what my father and I both envisioned.

One of the first things we did was start hiring the right people for critical roles. I promoted our superstar Marketing Manager to a director role, which freed me up to pursue other parts of the business, including business growth and development. He also helped me with some event planning and took over the sponsorship planning for some of the larger events. Now, I could start thinking about new ways to sell available markets to attorneys throughout the country.

As recently as four years ago, we were not really selling many new markets, but we were in the planning phase of figuring out the best sales and marketing strategy geared toward attorneys. We were having tremendous success on the consumer side in growing our motorcycle client intakes for our handful of attorney members; however, the other side of the business required alteration to attract additional qualified law firms to our program.

We continued to make improvements, and 2 1/2 years ago, I had the opportunity to purchase an additional ownership interest. Doing so gave me 50% ownership, equal to my father's, and I realized that this was my opportunity to transform our company and, ultimately, take it to the next level. For years, we had been using the same business-to-business techniques to try to attract new law firms. While our business-to-consumer business continued to grow and flourish by driving motorcycle clients to our existing members, we weren't making headway in adding new law firm members.

To be successful, I proposed that we needed fresh ideas and a multitiered approach. Quite frankly, we needed to employ our successful B2C marketing principles and practices to the B2B side of our business. It hit me one day when I was riding my motorcycle. The idea was simple; rather than showcase and market AAMIL, our member association, we needed to focus our B2B marketing through the lens of Law Tigers, taking the same multichannel marketing approach that we used for motorcyclists and utilizing it for attorneys.

One significant change was becoming a strategic sponsor at some of the large-scale lawyer conventions such as MTMP (Mass Torts Made Perfect) and NTL (National Trial Lawyers), smaller-scale trucking and brain injury seminars, and several targeted state trial lawyer association meetings. Rather than playing a vendor role as we had for the past decade, we selected highly visible brand sponsorships that included speaking slots, signage, material drops, and Wi-Fi branding. Once we started sponsoring events, we began to elevate the brand throughout the legal community. We began networking at these events and building meaningful relationships with other vendors, using the promoters' email list and attracting some of the country's top lawyers and law firms. Much like insurance and beverage companies had done at motorcycle events (and we followed suit), I wanted to implement the same brand-focused approach. There was no such thing as too much signage, and we always stood out and were highly engaged at our trade show booth. We put out drink coasters on all the tables and roll-up banners at the entrance and exit points and networked at every cocktail party and social event. This visibility made us look even bigger and more established than we were, and it showed lawyers that we were worth a look.

Another noteworthy change I implemented was hiring a seasoned business development professional. Instead of an average sales professional, of which we had several throughout the years, I wanted to focus on hiring someone who would increase sales and subsequently increase our growth. This change came at a considerable cost, but as they say, you need to spend money to make money. The person we hired had a different approach that was informative and consultant-like. Instead of sending out materials or cold calling, which doesn't work, he had a more consultative approach. With a program like ours (which can cost $500,000 to $1 million yearly for one market), the audience is more sophisticated and demanding. It was imperative to find the right person to represent Law Tigers on the sales end and to the lawyers buying into the program. Though the person who was with us during this first growth phase has since moved on, he played a key role in selling a dozen new markets. Two years ago, a new team member joined us to help us get to the next level. Through his creativity, professionalism, and incredible networking skills, we have been able to add another 25 markets. He utilized and leveraged technologies in the form of an e-book, articles, custom videos, and emails, helping educate prospective firms on how to be successful in creative and unique ways.

In the beginning, our challenge was that we only had a track record with my dad's firm. The program was hard to sell without the benefit of multiple firms showing long-term success with the program. Making these changes was a great way to build our visibility and solidify our brand presence. I realized that we also needed to change with the times and adapt our techniques to suit the digital age. During this time, I read a lot about email drip campaigns, e-books, educating, lecturing, and providing value to others. I understood the importance of speaking as an authority and a resource on niche marketing at numerous legal-related events.

We soon started utilizing these tools and resources, along with filming testimonials of both existing members and well-respected legal industry professionals who loved our program. Now that we had a couple of successful firms with a track record and data as evidence, we started to sell additional markets. Our efforts included citing changes and trends in the motorcycle industry concerning injury stats, injury severity, and market share. We provided this information in a way that showed investing in our program could be lucrative and sustainable. Using these tools and techniques, we created a new sales and marketing program to attract qualified law firms.

With these changes, we hypothesized that within the first year, we would sell three or four new memberships — and possibly another five or six in the second year. But much to our surprise, we started selling units quickly. In a matter of months, there was significant interest, and within the first three months, we had already sold four units.

Before I knew it, what I had always thought possible was finally a reality. I always knew we had an excellent program and a quality product. We just had to get it in front of the right people and show them that Law Tigers was worth investing in. By the end of that first year, we had sold a dozen markets. In many instances, firms bought multiple states and territories, which was not something I had initially anticipated, so it came as a surprise. Instead of buying one market and adding more over time, several firms were buying four or five at one time. One member is now up to 11 markets across the United States, and we have several others that are about to buy three to four. In their eyes, it simply made sense to scale and cover their bases with multiple territories or states. Then, when other existing members saw this happening, they purchased more markets before someone else bought them. We've experienced exponential growth with the addition of almost two dozen new markets this year with another 10 in the process of closing.

Law Tigers continues to transform and expand. To accommodate our growth, we have added to our team, improved our processes, and changed our infrastructure. Three years ago, we had a staff of three. Today, we have a corporate team comprised of 15 professionals, and within the next few months, we will be at 20. Additionally, we have 40 Marketing Managers employed by the local law firms, and we anticipate hiring an additional 10 team members within the next six months. Locally based, we recruit, manage, train, and supervise the Marketing Managers for our member law firms.

To be successful in business, you can't sit still. If you're not growing, you're dying! You mustn't be complacent, and you never rest on your laurels. What you've accomplished in the past isn't going to drive future success. You have to push yourself, get out of your comfort zone, surround yourself with talented team members who are more proficient than you are in their respective areas, and always look for opportunities to grow, improve, and offer more value. Whether it's with Law Tigers, motorcycle riders, or the motorcycle community at large, our goal is to continuously push ourselves, evolve, and be of service to our community.

Chapter

4

The Law Tigers Program

Law Tigers is an exclusive membership program that has similarities to a partnership. When you become part of Law Tigers, you are granted membership rights in the American Association of Motorcycle Injury Lawyers (AAMIL), an association comprised of successful, like-minded member law firms. While your member agreement is with AAMIL, we market the program under the Law Tigers brand.

Essentially, we license the intellectual property of the marketing program, along with all other aspects, such as the logo, taglines, advertising, and systems. As the program has grown, we have adapted our membership agreement to accommodate numerous improvements and changes. Opportunities to market the program, our offerings, and some of the terms in the contract continuously evolve.

When it comes to our program, we service two distinct clients — law firms and members of the motorcycle riding community and their loved ones. To our member law firms, we offer a turnkey marketing solution to address a need. In this case, it's to service an often-underserved population — the motorcycle community. The goal of our program is to provide value and support for riders and their family members, those who've been in an accident as well as those who've been riding without incident for years. The program functions as a resource prior, during, and after a motorcycle accident. Our member firms help their clients get their lives back on track and get back on their bikes if they're still inclined. Whatever the circumstances, we want our clients to get the treatment and compensation they deserve, and to assist them in any other way, so they're able to lead a productive life.

From the perspective of the law firms, the marketing model drives business within a tight-knit and extremely loyal community. The Law Tigers program is tailored to appeal to motorcycle riders and their family members. Our program provides operational training and assistance to ensure our member firms are equipped to handle motorcycle injury cases when riders need our services. This process begins well before a rider's injury through ubiquitous branding, community support and outreach, and an engineered and meticulously executed marketing strategy.

In most cases, law firms that have become part of our Law Tigers family couldn't quite figure out how to execute a successful marketing and advertising strategy geared toward riders because 1) they'd never advertised before, 2) they didn't know how to market to motorcyclists effectively, or 3) they didn't have the time, desire, or resources needed to develop a successful niche program within their existing practice. As a result, most had no idea how to create a formidable and sustainable motorcycle practice, which marketing techniques to implement, and which methods were the most effective in driving these opportunities — things ultimately necessary to lead to a successful motorcycle personal injury practice. For almost two decades, we have immersed ourselves in the rider culture and motorcycle industry. As motorcyclists ourselves, we know firsthand what resonates with our fellow riders, and we've used data and our experience to analyze industry trends, rider psychology, and lifestyle marketing. By partnering with a company like ours, there is no learning curve. We employ proven practices to get immediate positive results for our members.

I have encountered numerous law firms that have unsuccessfully marketed their services and wasted hundreds of thousands of dollars attempting to appeal to motorcyclists. In a nutshell, whether it was their generalist marketing strategies (which may have worked for their automotive practice) or their unsuccessful attempt to portray themselves as a rider, most never yielded positive results. With the level of competition, ever-rising advertising and marketing costs, and countless consumer touch points, it's simply too costly, time-consuming, and risky to try to develop a motorcycle practice on your own.

Often, firms implement a standard, conventional approach to marketing. These techniques usually include the use of generic television and billboard ads. While they may get a case here and there, they don't experience the volume of cases they were hoping for relative to their investment. In some cases, they may utilize various marketing tools but haven't done so effectively. For a marketing campaign to be successful, it must be holistic, involving a community component and resonating with riders on an emotional level. Instead of traditional marketing, you must find a way to speak to the audience directly when it comes to mass marketing, digital marketing, and grassroots marketing.

Old-fashioned, traditional principles of marketing may work for other fields, but it doesn't resonate with the motorcycle community. Unlike other personal injury clients, issues impacting the motorcycle community are vastly different. The legal approach to car accident cases or slip-and-fall cases based on negligence is vastly different. We help our members reach out and speak directly to the target audience.

For Law Tigers to be successful, we have implemented different practices, initiatives, and beliefs. Structurally, we offer a multichannel marketing strategy that involves connecting with riders in every aspect of the riding community. The holistic approach and means by which we implement and execute is our secret sauce. We don't just reach riders in one way but in many ways. This approach requires an operational structure; continuous training; new ideas and practices; hands-on support; one-on-one, peer, and team coaching; a clearly thought-out strategy; and talented individuals who can implement, manage, and execute all aspects of the program.

Our Vice President of Business Development and I examine data. When we approach a market, we gather and study relevant information, including the number of motorcycle injuries and fatalities that occur annually in any given state. Based on these figures, we have a tiered membership system. We also look at insurance laws, bar rules, and other state-by-state variables. From this information, we determine the value and viability of each market. Because we want our members to benefit from these opportunities, we don't sell small units or areas that provide a limited number of potential motorcycle clients. Often, the entire state is made exclusive to one firm to help ensure their success. There are only so many motorcycle accidents in any given market, splitting up the market and offering multiple units to different firms in some of the smaller or midsize states would not be a good investment. Larger states, such as California, Texas, Florida, New York, Tennessee, North Carolina, and Pennsylvania can have anywhere from two to six exclusive member territories. In these instances, there are a substantial number of annual motorcycle injuries and fatalities in each defined market within the state.

Each year, we attend industry shows, curate email drip campaigns, and create other content, such as white papers and e-books. When we attend lawyer conventions, I speak as an authority on niche marketing, especially within the motorcycle space. We continue to network with other businesses in the legal industry and utilize our existing firms as referral sources. Through these efforts, we find like-minded firms that want to help motorcycle riders and their community.

Firms that show interest in the Law Tigers program must align with our core beliefs and values. For us, it's not just about making money and taking in motorcycle cases. A potential Law Tigers firm must have consistent morals and values that align with ours. We meet with our firms face to face and require that they visit us to ensure we are a good fit for each other. Merely wanting to become a member of the Law Tigers program does not guarantee automatic admittance. It is a mutually agreed-upon decision and privilege.

To ensure that prospective firms are the right fit for our program, we have a stringent screening protocol. Not only do we look at whether a firm has any bar complaints, but we determine whether they are competent trial lawyers. If a firm representing the Law Tigers tries a case, we want them to be able to represent a rider with the highest level of care and commitment. We examine their operation, including their intake system, legal staff, and their overall firm infrastructure. We want to make sure they take good care of their team. Does their office culture meet our standards? We scrutinize all of these aspects, and if they don't align with our company's core mission and values, we won't partner with them.

We must make sure the firms we work with want to help people and have a similar vision. A potential Law Tigers firm has to be willing to put the client first and do it for the right reasons. We encourage our members to grow and improve. However, it's important to recognize that mistakes will happen. Often, when you are striving to improve, you'll have to take some calculated risks. You must be able to look at mistakes as a learning process. The right firm should be able to accept short-term failure, knowing that they'll yield long-term gains by being bold, unique, and willing to look at things from a different perspective.

The next step in the selection process includes ensuring prospective firms meet the criteria in terms of value, operations, lawyering skills, and finances. Buying into Law Tigers requires a sizable investment, so we must verify that potential firms have the necessary funding to properly grow and develop the program over the first two- to three-year startup period. Of course, we initially must make sure that the desired territory is available, as it is an exclusive opportunity.

In past instances, when a firm's first choice wasn't available, we would facilitate membership in an alternate state or territory in which they were licensed to practice. When we grant membership for a specific area, it's no longer available to another firm for the duration of the agreement. Once this entire vetting process is complete, we extend an offer for membership and continue with the next steps. A brief overview of a few program elements follows:

Program Offerings

- System utilization, immersion instruction, and on-site staff training
- Access to a specifically trained answering service
- Intake management tracking software
- Ongoing marketing and case intake management help
- The proven Law Tigers process and system

- Member relations, training, resources, networking events, and webinars
- National brand representation
- Use of membership marketing and operations manual
- Assistance in hiring, training, and ongoing marketing management
- Access to promotional products
- National and local website recognition
- Nationally recognized motorcycle hit-and-run and motorcycle theft program
- Access to high-value mass-marketing outlets

Chapter

5

The Benefits

The Law Tigers program offers a variety of benefits for our members. Not only do we provide support to help drive business, but we also provide them with exclusive access to our membership resources. Our members can benefit through collaboration, learning from experts, sharing ideas, and cross-referrals. Not only are these resources useful in making your firm more effective and client focused, but they also provide tools that will drive more business. One way we promote and facilitate these resources is by planning and hosting our members at our annual Law Tigers Motorcycle Lawyer Summit. For several days each year, we meet to learn from one another and outside experts, and we collaborate. During this event, there are ongoing opportunities to interact with other member firms, hear from expert witnesses, learn from business attendees who offer injury lawyer business services, and support and enjoy numerous other member-exclusive benefits.

In addition to our annual Lawyer Summit, AAMIL offers its members an online member portal with white papers, an email Listserv, instructional videos, expert witness resources, a monthly newsletter, and other educational tools.

We also provide our quarterly webinar series, offered exclusively to members, from which they can learn from vetted experts in a range of fields, including engineers, motorcycle safety specialists, surgeons, technology providers, life-care planners, trial consultants, and others. We facilitate an open dialogue and discussion session where members can share ideas about what is and isn't working for them. They address operational and marketing subject matter and discuss other topics with their fellow Law Tigers member firms from all over the country. Because we offer exclusive territories, our members aren't competing with each other. Instead, they support one another for the benefit of their market, firm, and the Law Tigers brand.

Lawyers go to law school and learn how to practice law and represent their clients; that's what they do best. On the other hand, Law Tigers is an organization that offers a unique program allowing members to market and support the motorcycle community. We don't represent clients. Our sole focus is to market Law Tigers on your behalf. We drive new business to firms so lawyers can continue to practice law and take care of their clients while providing firms with the opportunity to become an effective marketer in this competitive landscape.

In addition to the annual Law Tigers Lawyer Summit, we host a yearly Marketing Manager Summit. At this one-week summit in Phoenix, Law Tigers Marketing Managers and their Regional Marketing Directors from all over the country come together. They learn from each other, implement new programs and initiatives, and, ultimately, become more effective at driving grassroots motorcycle case referrals.

Law Tigers has 20 years of proven success. Not only does the program provide members with support from a national brand, but it also gives members a system and the tools and resources needed to become successful. As a member, you have access to every service we provide in our all-encompassing program, as outlined above. Members employ a Marketing Manager, who is tasked with curating a long-term, sustainable grassroots program directed to the riding community. We facilitate the hiring process, training, and ongoing management of this position. To penetrate the local market at every level, we offer a comprehensive training program that initially encompasses a one-year rollout followed by ongoing oversight and training supported with key performance indicators (KPIs), goals, and objectives.

Marketing Materials

As we look at every viable opportunity, the program involves visiting motorcycle shops and utilizing materials that we've developed and continue to add to each year. Our team produces useful materials in collaboration with motorcycle shops, including co-branded document holders, event and sales promotion flyers, and signage. We leverage our digital and traditional assets through social posts and contests, local radio, outdoor, and television promotions to help shops and dealerships.

The program includes sponsoring motorcycle events, as well as supporting clubs and organizations in numerous ways. Some of these initiatives include printing flyers, posters, and other printed assets for our event partners and producing educational and marketing materials for clubs and organizations. We manage all of the aspects of the program for our member firms, which allows the Marketing Manager to effectively and continually promote Law Tigers locally on behalf of the firm.

Our program includes a starter kit with the following trade show materials: branded tents, banners, blade flags, promotional items, a 20-foot inflatable Law Tigers logo, a mascot outfit, and other materials for use throughout the year. Our assigned Regional Marketing Director provides hands-on setup and execution training of the local Marketing Manager, who will be responsible for handling and using the event equipment.

We maintain a large inventory of field-tested promotional items in our warehouse that can be ordered by the Marketing Manager for shop visits, club meetings, and events. Many of these items are extremely popular and sought after, including our Tank plush toy, note pads, document wallet, Rider Benefit Card, and lip balm. Riders who attend motorcycle events ask for these and other Law Tigers items. We often use these giveaways as an incentive to obtain a rider's email address for future online marketing initiatives.

Additionally, we offer a variety of other useful resources and training to ensure the program's success. Further efforts include identifying motorcycle clubs and organizations to which we send materials and provide a host of services, including:

- Visiting these organizations and supporting them in a variety of ways, such as advertising in their newsletters, sponsoring their run or event, and printing co-branded marketing materials for their promotional use
- Providing education-based information and speaking at club meetings about insurance,

safety, what to do in an accident, and legal matters

- Establishing military-based partnerships in each market and speaking to riders on base about safety and insurance; in markets with a military population, we'll represent a large number of servicemen and servicewomen who are injured while riding their motorcycles

To further connect with consumers, we urge the local lawyers or their staff to periodically visit local shops, attend a few large events throughout the year, and speak to shop staff and club/organization members about a host of relevant topics.

Marketing Strategies

By implementing our grassroots marketing approach, we see these efforts generate a 30%-50% increase in new client business. By immersing ourselves in the riding community, supporting all aspects of the industry, helping riders in numerous ways, and addressing stakeholder needs, those who are part of the motorcycle industry refer their customers, friends, and loved ones to us. Often, many of these industry insiders are riders themselves, and they'll use us if they're ever injured. Our data shows that fellow riders, their family members, and members of motorcycle organizations commonly refer people to Law Tigers lawyers.

Over the years, we have developed a well-thought-out approach to working with and supporting the local community. Each market has a grassroots budget that the Marketing Manager uses to support motorcycle charity events, cover the cost of document holders, flyers, and other materials for shops and clubs, and sponsor large- and small-scale motorcycle events and runs. They also sponsor and attend local and national motorcycle race series, support bike nights, work with local tow companies and motorcycle training schools, and support dealer open houses.

Marketing Managers wearing Law Tigers attire and driving Law Tigers vans have shop visit routes they follow each week. They give the staff useful branded promotional items, such as notepads, pens, lip balm, counter mats, mousepads, and gloves, to name a few. During these shop visits, they build trust and develop a rapport that ultimately leads to client referrals.

Our program includes a comprehensive event-driven marketing strategy designed to maintain brand visibility among motorcycle riders. With the support of our Regional Marketing Director, the local Marketing Manager identifies both small and large events in which to participate. With an established annual event budget approved by each member law firm, the team identifies events to sponsor and attend, providing marketing materials for each one.

Law Tigers will participate in anywhere from 100-150 local motorcycle events in each market annually. Marketing Managers set up their branded Law Tigers booth and signage according to training standards to ensure maximum brand exposure. At these events, they'll distribute promotional items, capture email addresses, engage with riders, and promote our interests. Over time, this continuous interaction with the riding community, coupled with our ongoing support, results in an ever-present, powerful brand. The Marketing Manager transforms into a trusted advisor and community member with whom riders can relate to and count on. When riders need legal representation, Law Tigers is often the firm they call.

In addition to the grassroots component, members have access to our experienced in-house media buying department, in-house production team, and in-house digital department. Currently, we have two seasoned media buying professionals with over 35 years of combined experience in the field, along with six experienced digital team members. When it comes to traditional marketing — television, radio, print, and outdoor — we produce and place everything for our members internally with customized solutions to meet their local needs and requirements. Included as part of this service are highly produced and engaging lifestyle television spots, localized radio ads and rider talent endorsements, custom outdoor copy, and a series of print and digital ads for use in motorcycle publications.

We currently have over a dozen unique lifestyle television ads of various lengths from which to select. It's critical to choose an advertisement that fits the market in which the spot will air. Not only do we produce the ads and provide the necessary local tagging, but we also negotiate and place the media buy on behalf of our members. While it's the member's budget, we act as their agency. With our national footprint and excellent reputation, many years of media buying experience, and a large combined national budget, we negotiate rates that are much lower than what a local firm would pay on their own.

Because we pride ourselves on being relational rather than transactional, my Senior Media Buyer and I visit each new market for up to a week, meeting with all the television and radio stations and the outdoor companies. Doing so helps forge a personal relationship, which generally results in lower rates, more added value, lower preemption, and better spot placement.

As part of our service to our members, we produce our own outdoor creative and place the outdoor buy on their behalf. We also monitor the locations to ensure that trees don't block the view, the advertising rotates at an agreed-upon time frame, and that new locations are visible with a long read as motorists approach them. Once a budget is approved, we visit the market to assess which companies we'd like to work with and what strategy we'd like to employ. This plan includes placing boards in key locations that reach our target audience without compromising on achieving the greatest number of unique impressions at a hyper-efficient cost.

Our national purchasing power with the country's three largest outdoor companies and the fact that we advertise in 50 major markets allows us to drive down costs for the placement contracts. A majority of our competitors and other legal categories of advertisers only buy one market and don't have the experience, relationships, or leverage to compete at our level.

Another essential component of our marketing strategy is print advertising. In most instances, print is quickly becoming obsolete, but it is a valuable medium in certain circumstances. Law Tigers print ads are used in local and national motorcycle publications, motorcycle club and organization newsletters, motorcycle event guides, and motorcycle racing programs. The audience that subscribes to these print publications tends to represent an older segment of the riding population.

Often, these publications have online versions, along with newsletters and social media assets that we benefit from. We reach our younger and more tech-savvy riders through these digital platforms.

These highly targeted motorcycle publications continue to promote our brand, working with us to promote our articles, contests, and other content we want to share with their subscribers and members.

We truly operate like a private, in-house marketing agency that services a limited number of successful law firms. Our team members are the best in the business and are committed to providing the highest level of customer service to our members. They are professional yet tough when it comes to negotiating and holding our media vendors accountable.

Not only do we work within the budget determined by our members, but we monitor these efforts and negotiate every initiative. Members can rely on us to represent their best interests in various ways: TV commercial airing credits, added value, monthly posting, optimal outdoor rotation, securing unobstructed billboard views, and billboard override. We drive rates down and frequently get more added value than our competitors. We fight for our members every step of the way to get the most value and exposure, which then drives business and translates into cases. This is why Law Tigers employs experienced traditional, grassroots, and digital professionals. Our team gets rates and sponsorships our members would never be able to secure on their own (or through a conventional advertising agency).

When we sell a market, our Senior Media Buyer and I schedule an on-site visit, both to get an idea of the market conditions and variables and to start the relationship development process. For up to a week, we meet with all the outdoor companies, television stations, and radio stations within that member's market. While it's time-consuming and expensive, it's something that we're committed to doing. One of our core beliefs is to be relational rather than transactional. During these meetings, we are evaluating which company is the best fit. We can look them in the eye, go for lunch, and learn about each other from both a personal and professional perspective.

Most agencies and companies communicate with radio stations, TV stations, and outdoor companies via email and phone. We pride ourselves on really getting to know the staff and their managers personally, which, in turn, translates into better representation, more added value, lower rates, preferential placements and upgrades, and better overall service.

Unlike other agencies, Law Tigers is able to utilize digital, traditional, and grassroots resources in a host of ways to support our partners. We pride ourselves on leveraging partnerships to help others in the industry, which ultimately benefits our members.

For example, if you're a race promoter, a motorcycle dealer, a charitable organization, or an event promoter, part of our negotiation with these media companies includes providing additional value and exposure to our partners. If there's a motorcycle race or other event we are sponsoring, as we do in many markets, we will use the local outdoor company's available inventory to get free or highly discounted digital or static billboards to promote the race. We already have a relationship with all three national outdoor companies and several dozen local ones throughout the country, so we're able to either receive bonus or highly discounted inventory at or below what we pay for our season-long campaigns. As a result, we can help promoters drive ticket sales for their races and other motorcycle events.

And if we are advertising with a radio station, we have motorcycle celebrities and local DJs cut promotional spots, facilitate contests and ticket giveaways, make on-site appearances, and conduct in-studio interviews and promotions. This advertising helps bring brand awareness and drive sales to help our event partners, charities, dealerships, and other organizations with whom we work or support.

In many of our markets, we leverage our television buys to include lifestyle segments that allow us to film our partners in-studio and on-site at the event for a broad audience to see. We'll conduct interviews with the major local television affiliates and sports networks during pregame shows. Often, they'll give us bonus spots or highly discounted inventory a month or two before an event that we support or sponsor. Of course, the Law Tigers logo and participation are also referenced in these commercials, so viewers are aware of our association and sponsorship of the event. Stations, such as Fox Sports, Root Sports, and AT&T Sports, often donate their professional sports franchise suites and tickets for us to give away to the public for promotional use or as a way to entertain our clients, business partners, and shop staff.

Whether it's to assist local charities, motorcycle dealerships, other motorcycle industry businesses, or event promoters, we provide our members with resources and publicity that would be expensive or even impossible for them to do on their own. As a result, our industry partners find immense value in our services. They are more inclined to refer clients, offer lower sponsorship costs, and show their loyalty through exclusive partnerships. Being able to leverage relationships is a significant benefit to our law firm members and local motorcycle industry partners.

If our members tried to implement these programs and initiatives independently, they would have to pay tens of thousands of dollars for the value that we provide for free or for pennies on the dollar. For the benefit of our law firm members, we place value in building relationships, negotiating packages, and leveraging spending. We determine what's important to both the local riding community and our local motorcycle industry partners. Our expertise comes from years of experience learning how to best utilize our assets and resources for the benefit of our members, riders, and industry partners.

Digital and Web Support

As a full-service, turnkey program, we offer an experienced digital department comprised of six digital professionals. All our team members, including those in digital, are focused exclusively on our members' Law Tigers marketing efforts. We eliminate the need to hire an agency or other third-party providers that don't have their best interests in mind. Often, these contractors have no idea how to market to the motorcycle community, have too many clients to service, and are understaffed.

The Law Tigers digital team is devoted exclusively to providing their services to our group of members. They understand what resonates with riders and focus on ways to drive business to our firms. Our team continually improves our website functionality, design, content, and user experience. Their focus includes making sure that our logos are correctly used as per our branding guidelines, updating and customizing our print, digital, and outdoor creative, and supporting all of the creative and advertising needs of our members.

Our team includes a full-time Video Producer, SEO Strategist, Content Manager, Social Media Manager, Graphic Designer, and Director of Digital Marketing. Each role is unique and requires a specific skill set to meet our goals and objectives.

Our Video Producer films on location at motorcycle events and races throughout the country. This content is used for social media and for promoting past and future events. It's essential to convey that we are a lifestyle brand and a community resource. We use this footage to share relevant content with riders and assist our event partners by creating commercials for digital and traditional use to promote the event the following year.

To help support our members, we include a visit to the firm to film our attorney members answering FAQs, giving client testimonials, collaborating with their team, riding in and out of the office, and participating in client appreciation events. We use this video for content on their local landing pages and social media. While we are a national brand, we establish a local presence and employ locally driven initiatives in each of our markets. It's essential to showcase local clients, local events and activities, local content, and our local law firms.

These initiatives are planned and executed by several of our team members who collaborate closely with each law firm member's staff. Our Content Manager is responsible for coordinating our digital projects, working with our influencers, and writing content and overseeing our blog, web content, contests, and newsletters, just to highlight a few.

Our Digital Strategist has numerous job functions, including running our multimillion-dollar pay-per-click (PPC) program, overseeing over 100 Google My Business listings, developing and implementing multiple SEO initiatives, and maintaining both our business and consumer websites.

To meet the ongoing content needs on our social media platforms and develop additional partnerships with influencers and other motorcycle businesses, we have a Social Media Manager. He is responsible for creating motorcycle content, campaigns, and partnerships. He works closely with our Content Manager on strategy, posting schedules, our blog, articles for magazines and newsletters, and co-branded campaigns and contests.

For all graphic requests, including print and digital ads, landing pages, website layouts and imagery, logos, newsletters, and all other image-related needs, we have a talented graphic designer and web developer. With requests coming from 40 markets and counting, there are numerous ad insertion requests, contest landing pages, website changes, billboard and print ad localization requirements, and countless ongoing updates to keep our brand consistent and top of mind with riders throughout the country.

Overseeing the digital department is our Director of Digital Marketing, who works with me directly on establishing the team and individual goals and objectives. He also works closely with our traditional and grassroots teams to support their initiatives and ensure that his department is leveraging their resources and assets in a way that maximizes brand awareness and lead generation and conversion. We pride ourselves on leading the way as an innovator in the digital marketing and networking arena within the motorcycle market vertical. Law Tigers members have an entire team of digital professionals at their disposal whose sole focus is using all our resources and expertise to drive as many motorcycle accident leads as we can to our member firms.

All our members have access to a comprehensive, specialized, and dedicated team of digital professionals who will meet all their needs. They work to help us grow, differentiate, and speak to our audience — riders and their loved ones. If members had to invest in these services, they would be paying hundreds of thousands of dollars. Even then, they couldn't match the specialization of the Law Tigers team. We are unique and highly specialized because we serve our own and are part of the motorcycle community. With a third party, you would just end up being one among many clients. At Law Tigers, we've taken every service and every component that can provide value to our members and made it a priority. We offer our white glove service exclusively to our members and no one else.

Client Relations

Firms often focus their time and energy entirely on marketing and advertising at the expense of their existing or former clients. Happy clients refer other clients, and putting a little time and effort into a client relations program can drive as much as 20%-30% more cases to your firm. As an added benefit to our members, Law Tigers has a dedicated Client and Member Relations Manager who focuses time and energy on supporting our attorney members through various key initiatives and programs.

For example, we host an annual Law Tigers Member Summit where members meet for two days to share ideas, listen to experts within the motorcycle industry and in practice development, and learn from each other how to become more efficient, effective, and profitable. Our Client and Member Relations Manager is responsible for planning and coordinating all aspects of this event. The role includes visiting every firm to learn about each firm's culture, intake and case management processes, client relations initiatives, and other systems to share the best practices with our member law firms. We are in the process of integrating HubSpot, a marketing technology solution, with our members' intake and case management software, which will allow us to pull and analyze data to find trends and opportunities. Some of these include ways to more efficiently market, increasing average fees, improving on the client experience, and enhancing cash flow.

The Client and Member Relations Manager also ensures that our Video Producer and Content Manager can produce the necessary written and video content for our website, landing pages, and social media. A principal responsibility beyond those already mentioned includes bringing new ideas to our firms, suggesting ways to increase referrals from former and existing clients through our bimonthly newsletter. We facilitate these goals with additional client touches, such as birthday and holiday cards, client appreciation kits, and regularly scheduled client appreciation events and activities.

Community/Industry Relations

This team member is responsible for developing strategic motorcycle industry partnerships and working with other motorcycle businesses and our well-known brand ambassadors to initiate contests, encourage cross-referrals, and engage their audience. This executive curates press releases and promotes our brand across multiple channels. In addition, he shares with riders, the motorcycle industry, and the press the many ways we support the riding community. Another key responsibility is interfacing with our local Marketing Managers' contacts in over 40 markets by leveraging their local shops, clubs, events, and influencer contacts to push out content through their marketing channels. Between our national and local resources, we can reach tens if not hundreds of thousands of riders and their families in a targeted and effective manner.

Operational Support

Operations Director and Operations Associate

Law Tigers offers significant operational support through our Director of Operations and Operations Assistant positions. This team supports our members' success by handling requests and ensuring our members have everything they need to be successful. Their responsibilities range from ordering and maintaining promotional item inventory, facilitating promotional product purchase orders, and ensuring our software and systems are working properly to overseeing all our accounting needs. The backbone of our organization, our operations team, provides our members with the highest level of service. They make sure that our equipment and promotional inventory is kept stocked, items on order are fulfilled to our members, all invoices are paid, and all systems and processes are followed. Whether it's onboarding new staff or supporting our programs and initiatives, they ensure the program runs smoothly, and they keep our law firm members and AAMIL team members happy.

Vice President of Field Operations

In 2019, we decided that it was time to take our company to the next level by providing our law firm and team members with additional support. To improve processes and drive even more cases, we needed to hold our AAMIL field team members to an even higher standard. As a result, I created the Vice President of Field Operations position to oversee our entire grassroots division, including all five of our Regional Marketing Directors and 40 local Marketing Managers. His responsibilities include negotiating and running all of our national and regional events and race series sponsorships, overseeing and planning our numerous contests and sweepstakes, initiating our new member grassroots market launches, interfacing with the traditional and digital department managers, and managing our entire team of 45 field-marketing professionals. Through the implementation of Salesforce and with continuous training, dialogue, assessments, and in-person visits, he has transformed our team and organization. Under the Vice President of Field Operations and Regional Marketing Directors leadership, our dedicated Marketing Managers have become highly skilled and effective at fostering meaningful relationships that result in countless direct motorcycle accident referrals to our member firms.

Regional Marketing Directors

Another essential element of the Law Tigers program includes our Regional Marketing Directors. They're the liaison between AAMIL and the member firms within the territories they oversee. Currently, we have five team members in this role, each responsible for a different region. We anticipate the need for another two within the foreseeable future, based on our growth throughout the country.

Every quarter, the Regional Marketing Directors visit the eight to 10 markets they oversee, spending time with the local Marketing Manager within that territory. During their visits, they meet with the lawyer and their staff and address any questions they have. However, they spend most of their time with the Marketing Manager, visiting shops, attending events, meeting with their club contacts, and ensuring adherence to our program. Through systems we've developed, we can analyze whether they're meeting their KPIs and their other goals and objectives.

Additionally, the Regional Marketing Directors ensure that they attend the required number of events, follow proper event setup protocol, and appropriately distribute marketing materials to rider attendees. They listen to how their managers approach and address potential industry referral sources, providing them with feedback on how to grow and improve. Essentially, they are making sure that the Marketing Manager follows the program, gets the necessary support, and ensures they have the tools they need to help drive motorcycle leads.

During quarterly visits, our Regional Marketing Directors meet with the local member firm to keep them apprised of our extensive local grassroots efforts, which effectively drive a significant number of motorcycle cases. These efforts include calls, shop visits, event participation, clubs/organization outreach, industry partnerships, emails, and tracking/management systems.

To ensure accountability, our Regional Marketing Directors enable GPS tracking of their Marketing Manager's Law Tigers vans to confirm they are in the field, completing their routes, and using Salesforce, our customer relationship management (CRM) software. This platform tracks and monitors all of the contacts and data entered into the system, including shop visits, events, budgets, inventory, club contacts, and all other activities. Not only does it keep the managers accountable, but it allows the Directors to keep track of their local progress.

Legacy Benefits

An attractive feature of the Law Tigers program is that it provides legacy benefits. The reputation lies with the brand. By relying on the brand to drive business and support your firm, you can have people working on behalf of the firm handle these cases. Essentially, the brand outshines and outlives the individual. From a legacy or retirement standpoint, you could pass it on to younger associates and recoup some of your original investment or sell it to another firm down the road. This option could provide an excellent retirement program for our members. In fact, we currently have three father-and-son member firms who recognized the value of Law Tigers in creating a lasting legacy.

Generally, when a lawyer owns an injury law firm, it is typically in their name, and the value of the firm is based on the cases currently in inventory. When a lawyer decides to retire, they are generally bought out based on the prorated value of that existing inventory. Because our program is a renewable 30-year program, our member owns the brand equity for their area and can capitalize on this financially.

Once the brand is established, cases will continue to come in, and revenue can be predicted within a specific range, enhancing the value of the law firm associated with the membership rights of the program. The legacy benefit also serves as a salable asset that generates cases, having greater value than a firm that's simply under an attorney's name. Ultimately, the program has an inherent transferable value. The original individual or practice group that purchased it can cash out at a substantial return.

The Collective Team

Law Tigers is comprised of a team of experienced and dedicated professionals who genuinely understand the motorcycle community. All the Directors and most of the Marketing Managers are riders themselves. Not only do they work to service and serve the motorcycle community, but they're also part of it. They understand what it takes; they live and breathe it.

The members also have me. Not only am I a rider, but I'm the Chief Operating Officer and co-owner. I've been in the business for 20 years. I'm a working owner, someone who's very hands on. I visit the markets, meet with members, attend events, produce content, and continuously look for ways for my team and me to grow and improve. I enjoy interacting with the lawyers, the Directors, the Marketing Managers, the industry partners, and the riding community. While my role has shifted to be more of a thought leader and strategist, I make sure we never rest on our laurels. While I continue to run and oversee the day-to-day operations, having a skilled group of dedicated team members makes my job much easier and more enjoyable.

On that note, I never worry about the limited competition. In fact, competition can be good. It's been the impetus to drive us to make improvements, think outside the box, and do things much differently than we ever would have. We've had to create opportunities that didn't exist, which have allowed the Law Tigers to dominate market share throughout the country.

For example, we had an experience with a specific event we used to sponsor. The promoter wasn't providing the level of service or value we expected and deserved. My competitor came in and offered four times more for an event that we had sponsored and had first right of refusal for. We didn't counter the offer (and weren't given the opportunity to do so). We could have flexed our legal muscles; however, it wasn't worth the time or expense.

We lost the official sponsorship and affiliation with the event, driving us to think outside the box to achieve our objectives. In this case, we had to get more creative, which made us more effective in the long run. We created a phrase for taking things into our own hands through creativity, strategic initiatives, and guerilla marketing at these events that we didn't sponsor for one reason or another. We refer to it as "Banditing the Event" — taking matters into our own hands by placing signage (banners, billboards, inflatables, and vehicles) around the perimeter of the venue and the area leading up to it. It also means working directly with local restaurants, bars, gas stations, campgrounds, and other businesses within or outside the venue to make it appear as if we are somehow involved in the event, even if we aren't. We've run digital promotions and contests that make it look as if we are a sponsor of the event when we aren't. It's been so successful throughout the country that we now employ these same tactics with all events, including those we do sponsor. Doing so provides us with additional branding and exposure beyond what the event promoter includes with our sponsorship package.

When we do sponsor events, we push the limits and treat the budget provided to us like it was our own. My team and I are skilled negotiators, and we can get more than other sponsors for a fraction of the price. After doing this for 20 years, I've learned (and taught my team) how to obtain the most value out of sponsorships. Some of these elements include numerous event tickets, television exposure, unlimited on-site signage and branding, prime placement of tents and inflatables, top tier television and radio advertising, and extensive digital coverage.

I make sure we are always pushing the limits and looking for new ways to be relevant, providing value to riders and members toward owning their share of the U.S. motorcycle injury market. As long as we stick to our game plan, no one can stop us. We continually progress, evolve, and improve. We can't worry about what other people are doing. If we do the best we can and never rest, we'll have success, and so will our members.

Additionally, my father, our CEO and founder, is still involved with the agreements, intellectual property, and oversight of our entire Law Tigers program.

He manages his own law firm with the membership rights to Arizona, Utah, New Mexico, San Diego, and Southern California's Inland Empire: Orange, Riverside, and San Bernardino Counties. His expertise and knowledge base of our entire marketing and operations system, along with his experience as a business lawyer, makes him a critical part of our organization. As the founder of AAMIL, his law firm, Levenbaum and Trachtenberg, was the first Law Tigers member. He created this program, and he and I developed it into what it is today. His leadership, vision, and management are the reasons why we have been so successful over the years.

The Law Tigers brand is highly regarded, respected, and well known across the country. Riders and their families have come to love and trust our brand, and we do whatever is necessary to protect it. We are diligent in ensuring that all our brand marks and intellectual property are up to date. We protect what's valuable from competitors and copycats by upholding and protecting our intellectual property, thus maintaining our originality and value. Given the level of investment and commitment from our members, along with our desire to protect them and their interests, we go to great lengths to keep others from stealing our ideas, processes, and intellectual property.

Chapter

6

Culture

Any successful business that is able to stand the test of time relies heavily on culture. Fostering a positive culture involves putting the team first, valuing your staff members, and recognizing good work.

When I first got involved in the company, I really didn't think about culture or what it meant. Initially, I was my father's employee and not in a position to dictate who we were or what we believed in as a company. As we grew, I realized just how important it was to attract and hire the right team and initiate policies and practices that fostered a positive, rewarding, and productive environment.

While I'm not perfect or claim to have all of the answers, I can tell you that I have a dedicated team focused on serving our members and the riding community. I know that I can count on each and every one of them — they have my back, and I have theirs.

When I was a teacher, I was able to interact with all types of students, recognizing their learning styles and personalities, relating to each of them accordingly. With this experience, I came to understand the importance of providing an environment that was safe and educational and acknowledging hard work. As a teacher, I focused on collaboration, validation of opinions, and support for students who struggled by offering extra time and effort to help them succeed. This foundation and mindset helped me see ways to improve the culture and use what I had learned to elevate the environment once I started working full time with Law Tigers.

At that time, AAMIL only had two or three employees and was housed in the same office as my dad's law firm. Quiet, compartmentalized, and conventional, AAMIL didn't reward innovation, encourage continuous learning, or acknowledge a job well done but functioned in a traditional, top-down, old-school way, as it had for years.

While this approach worked on a small scale, I sensed that something was missing and began to think of ways to do things differently — to implement change and become more employee focused. To my dad's and several members of his long-term staff's credit, the law firm has also made numerous positive changes since then, and I know some of what I have done with AAMIL has positively impacted my father and his law firm.

I began reading about culture and the benefits of being proactive, valuing your staff, and being more consultative. Along the way, I met with several business coaches and successful business owners whom I admired to learn more about what made them successful and how they were able to scale their business.

After working as an employee for 12 years, I was fortunate to become an owner, which allowed me to shift my role and the direction of the company to help promote growth and sustainability. When I had the opportunity to build a team and create a culture, I implemented a number of strategies and business tactics that I had learned. Essentially, I wanted to treat people the way that I wanted to be treated, which involved getting feedback from everyone regarding ideas and decisions that had to be made. Not only did I want to make decisions based on what I thought was right, but I also wanted other opinions and insight. While it may take longer to get things done, this method fosters a culture of teamwork and collaboration that improved productivity and enhanced morale.

A key aspect of the culture and environment I created involves recognizing accomplishments and rewarding effort and good work. Our company encourages people to take time off when they have it. We offer 3 1/2 weeks of personal time, adding an additional five days after working with us for five years. I want employees to spend time with their family, recharge, and not feel guilty about downtime. I also wanted to foster a culture that rewards risk taking. While we are results-driven, the focus is not on how many hours go into a task. I want to make sure that employees are being productive and encourage quality over quantity. Essentially, we focus on valuing the individual and giving them the support they need to be successful.

To work collaboratively, we facilitate regularly scheduled leadership team meetings. At these meetings, the team from the corporate office meets with the Regional Marketing Directors. Together, we address numerous aspects of our operations and make decisions based on thoughtful discussion and debate, ultimately reaching a consensus. Whether it's sponsorships, strategic changes, or idea sharing, we decide as a team. I do not make singular decisions based on my position as the owner but, instead, encourage my team to question me. If they don't agree with something, they can voice their opinion without fear of repercussion or punishment.

We have created a culture of collaboration, mutual respect, and teamwork. While recognizing individuality and encouraging individual merits, we also strive to continue to learn and grow. I believe self-improvement is necessary to evolve and become more successful. Fostering this culture has made us successful. By empowering my staff to make decisions and take chances, I allow them to think outside the box and take ownership of their ideas.

I have learned how to surround myself with people who are smarter than me and more experienced in their respective areas. Whether it's our media buyers, the directors, the marketing managers, the digital team, or the operations staff, all of these people are exceptionally good at what they do, and they make me look good. I have no problem knowing they are more knowledgeable or capable in certain aspects of their role; in fact, that's exactly what I am looking for. A sign of a good leader is hiring people who have a set of skills you don't possess. My job is to be a facilitator — a thought leader — and my focus is to ensure my teams feel emboldened, empowered, motivated, and supported.

Not only has this philosophy made us successful, but it has also attracted firms that have similar viewpoints. All our member law firms are extremely progressive. They are employee focused as well as client focused. Their beliefs and initiatives are consistent with ours, which has allowed both of us to grow. When we encounter a firm that fosters a similar culture and is successful, it just makes sense for us to work together. When they want to take on another practice area — in this case, motorcycle personal injury — the collaboration is mutually beneficial. Not only do these kinds of firms represent the Law Tigers brand in an exemplary manner, but they also function as an extension of us and what we represent. When done properly, it's a powerful and effective tool to help transform a local motorcycle law firm into a formidable powerhouse motorcycle injury brand that millions of riders and their families are aware of.

To ensure long-term success, the highest level of performance, and retention of staff and our member firms, sustaining our culture is the most important thing I can do. When employees are fulfilled, valued, and appreciated, they are going to perform well. They're also going to want to improve and do right by you. And I want to do right by them as well. Culture permeates everything we do. While some organizations overlook or diminish its importance, for us, culture is a priority.

A large part of our culture involves giving back to the community. One such initiative involves all our staff taking one workday off to donate time and effort to a cause or charity. We allow our team members the opportunity to do something on their own and give back to the community.

We ensure that everyone signs up for at least one seminar or participates in a growth-type activity each year, giving employees opportunities to enrich and educate themselves on ways to improve, both professionally and personally. We cover all related costs for participating in a volunteer capacity or professional growth activity of their choice.

As an entire team, we take part in a community-related activity during one workday each year. Last year, we worked together at a food bank and a women's shelter, and we're trying to do something with Habitat for Humanity this year. I believe in investing in our team and the community and giving team members that opportunity for lifelong learning.

In addition to our AAMIL team's charity and learning initiatives, each of our Marketing Managers supports and participates in dozens of local motorcycle charity-related events to support their local community. Whether it's veteran's groups, animal rescue shelters, women's shelters, children's hospitals, or the countless other organizations in which we are involved, the Law Tigers team will always give back to those who are less fortunate and in need of help.

Language

As I continue to read about the importance of culture, I have discovered the importance of having a common language and living it every day. This language not only applies to customer service and how we treat staff, but it also applies to colleagues, peers, and the public. An interesting aspect of AAMIL's language is our use of catchphrases.

I discovered that many successful companies have their own language and colloquialisms. Not only do these words become part of their vernacular, but they live and breathe their vocabulary every day. Catchphrases teach and reinforce lessons to new and existing staff while providing that same value to their customers and the general public.

Several years ago, I decided that we should come up with our own catchphrases. Some of the ones we came up with were already extensively used; we just hadn't formalized them. Through this exercise, the leadership team was able to collaborate, flush out our core values, and determine what we wanted to adopt as part of our everyday language. The goal was to reinforce our story, values, culture, successes, and best practices.

We decided on eight catchphrases based on experiences we've had, our belief system, teachable moments, and values that we want to reinforce.

1. *"Bandit the Event!"*

When I came on board 20 years ago, the Arizona Bike Week event was just getting a foothold, and "Bandit the Event!" came about as a result of things that happened there. My dad had told me that it was the biggest event in Arizona and that we had to participate in it. Unfortunately, we were met with resistance from the promoters because they gave another lawyer exclusivity at the time.

I've never been okay with being told I can't do something, especially when I didn't believe the response was fair or reasonable. We had recently acquired an A-frame mobile billboard — essentially a two-sided billboard on a trailer. I then came up with the idea to "bandit" the event, which means that in cases where the promoter will not let us in, we will use guerilla marketing and other techniques to gain visibility and get value from the event.

To "bandit" that event, I parked the A-frame on the side of an access road leading into the venue and left it there all weekend.

Despite not being welcomed by the promoter, on the last day of the event, he asked me to move the trailer, and as a concession for moving it, he agreed to let us into the event the following year. We went in and moved the trailer, got into the event the next year, and the rest is history.

We are now a major sponsor of that event as well as a partner in helping to promote it. I am good friends with the promoter (we ride to Sturgis together). We provide traditional, digital, and grassroots support to the event each year through a well-thought-out, fully integrated marketing strategy. As a result, we get a ton of added value and additional exposure compared to other sponsors. This year, we will be onstage showcasing a custom bike build we sponsored with a veteran's organization in front of 30,000 riders just before the headliner band comes on. The association with this amazing organization and the exposure we'll get from being onstage was not part of our contract. It resulted from our deep-rooted relationship with the promoter and going above and beyond to support the event.

2. *"Be Relational, NOT Transactional"*

Our next catchphrase, "Be Relational, NOT Transactional" is one that has become vital to our business. In fact, I'd consider it our rallying cry! We practice and preach these words when negotiating and working with a sponsor, promotor, or club. In most cases, we're not going to necessarily be the ones who are willing to write the biggest check, especially compared to our wannabe competitors. In some cases, we have even lost out on events that we were once involved in because a competitor is willing to offer more than we could justify.

However, because of the way our program is structured, we offer the value that goes beyond a check. Not only do we approach these events intent on creating a valuable partnership, but we also want to connect with other individuals in this industry and help their business thrive. In addition to helping sell tickets and drive attendance, we want to bring awareness to their event and offer support. Companies that focus on the transactional aspect of a deal simply write a check, wipe their hands, and expect something in return.

We focus on the relationship aspect of a partnership that guarantees a mutually beneficial outcome. With this approach, it's a win-win for both parties involved. This catchphrase permeates our culture, business model, and belief system. Being relationship focused and driven by what's best for both parties is something I have always practiced over the years. As a result, we have become a resource within the community and have developed meaningful relationships.

3. *"Everything Is Earned"*

This catchphrase draws focus on our hard work and drive. One of the main reasons we are successful is because we work hard and put value into everything we do. For example, sometimes a competitor will sponsor an event, put their names on it, and just show up. My team has a list of tasks and deliverables to drive awareness and engagement that includes a significant amount of signage and branding on-site, as well as digital and traditional promotion. But a lot of it also comes down to cultivating relationships and providing value. My teams, especially my Managers and Directors, put in long hours and work many weekends. For us, it's not just a job; it's a lifestyle. While nothing comes easy, we work hard, push ourselves, and we're not afraid to get our hands dirty.

4. *"It's a Marathon, Not a Sprint"*

Essentially, we believe there are no shortcuts in business. When we do something, we take our time and do it right. Whether it's enhancing our brand or going into a new market, nothing happens overnight. Our Law Tigers program generally takes two to three years to fully mature, then lasts for countless years. The program is designed to operate successfully, but the numerous components that drive business need time to mature. As the brand develops, you have to build trust and respect within the community. In all aspects of our business, if you're patient, the clients will come.

Some people believe that the simple act of putting up a commercial, running a print advertisement, or sponsoring an event will drive business and be enough for a company to succeed. This perception couldn't be more wrong. Driving business is a culmination of numerous opportunities, relationship building, and long-term branding efforts. It doesn't simply happen because of one technique. Anyone who wants to be successful in any business can't expect quick results.

It takes time for a brand to make an impact and get noticed. Most people need to see something eight times before it sticks. They need to see it in multiple areas

and through different mediums before it truly stands out. Additionally, consumers must have a good experience with a brand and have that positive association. Rather than just expecting the brand itself to do all the work, you must engage and interact with your target audience.

5. *"We Ride as One"*

This catchphrase encompasses our shared vision and overall mission. Because we value teamwork and collaboration, we work to support each other. Instead of punishing someone for making a mistake, we work together to help correct it. We encourage people to learn and grow from the experience. In our business, there's no fear of retribution or punishment. We empower one another and work as a team. Together, we are stronger.

6. "Make the Logo Bigger!"

We selected this catchphrase because it is something that I am always saying. For me, the brand is critically important. Not only that, but I also want us to stand out. When people outside the organization don't have a clear understanding of what we stand for or who we are, we must correct it. There have been times when I've seen our logo in an advertisement and it's hard to make out or read. In most cases, the partner, promoter, or publisher doesn't understand the value of our logo being visible and standing out. Anytime we do a deal or sponsor an event, we want to stand out and make sure that our brand is visible and bold. In my opinion, the logo can never be too big. The bigger, the better! Whether in print, digital, or on signage, our focus is on branding, visibility, and standing out, just like Coca-Cola or Nike.

7. "Be the Resource"

This catchphrase succinctly captures our vision. As I've mentioned, we want to be THE resource the motorcycle community turns to when in need. While we are an association that markets on behalf of our member law firms, we are a lifestyle brand that is an integral part of the riding community. Not only do we support riders, but we also support businesses within this industry. As a result, we are embraced by dealerships, manufacturers, and other organizations within the motorcycle community. Not only do we implement this approach within the community, but we also apply this within our own company, encouraging staff to become resources for one another.

8. *"Have Fun Getting It Done"*

Ultimately, it's about having a good time and making money, too. Members of our team are part of this program because they love motorcycles, and they love the culture within the riding community. For us, it's not a job; it's a passion. While the hours can be long and the work can be hard, we all enjoy what we do. We achieve our goals and objectives, and we have a good time doing it. What makes us successful is the balance of both — having fun and getting it done.

We created these catchphrases to utilize a language that embodies our culture. By reinforcing our values and beliefs through a common language, we can stay true to what's important and continue to foster a positive culture.

Chapter

7

The Motorcycle Community

Law Tigers is unique because we serve a specific niche community — motorcycle riders. For us, knowledge of the riding community is critical. Our goal is to help riders and their loved ones, along with motorcycle organizations and businesses, in any way we can. To do this successfully, we need to understand who they are as well as their wants and needs. While the community is unique in and of itself, within the community, there are different subsets.

We must first look at what motivates someone to start riding to understand these differences. In this case, there are two groups: those who choose a motorcycle as an economical mode of transportation and those who ride because they love how it feels and what it represents. Of course, some riders fit into both categories.

The first group of people is usually motivated by financial reasons. Motorcycles are less expensive than automobiles in a variety of ways. The cost of insuring and fueling a motorcycle cuts costs that would be associated with buying and maintaining a car. Members of this group would be considered practical-use riders, but they also enjoy riding. In the end, it takes a certain kind of person to ride a motorcycle, regardless of motivation. To be a rider, you must be willing to take some calculated risks, as it is potentially dangerous.

The second group is comprised of individuals who may also use their motorcycle for transportation reasons, but they mainly ride because it is a way of life, a lifestyle, for them. Riding a bike is a much different experience than being in a car because there are no creature comforts or the safety, calm, and protection offered by the surrounding frame of an automobile.

When you're riding on a motorcycle, you're constantly engaged and must always be aware of your surroundings. You're balanced on a narrow seat and exposed to all the elements: bugs, wind, noises and the sounds of nature, man, and machine. Riding is an interactive, stimulating experience.

This experience is what appeals to people who love to ride. It's not stagnant or numbing. When you're driving a car, you get into a typical mode, zone out, and drive to your destination. A car is used as a means of getting from point A to point B. On a bike, it's all about the experience. It's not just about getting somewhere; it's about the journey. Often, you'll see people riding motorcycles without a destination in mind. They just jump on their bike and ride because they crave the sensory experience you can't get in a car. With a bike, you're in control. You lean. You turn. You react. You're one with the machine.

Being a rider encompasses something you don't experience in most motorized modes of transportation. All these elements are very appealing for people who want to feel the mind/body experience that comes with being on a motorcycle. In addition to the experience, there are other variables. Bikes are reactive. Some bikes will beat a Ferrari or other high-performance sports cars. Not everybody can afford a $200,000 car, but you can get a similar experience on a motorcycle. For a fraction of the cost, not only do you get an adrenaline rush with the responsiveness and speed of a race car, but you can likewise accelerate quickly and make swift movements.

Riding appeals to people who are free-spirited, open to taking chances, and desire a fulfilling life. Within the community, riders tend to be incredibly positive people who want to take control of their lives. They are like-minded individuals who are not sheltered or afraid. They crave adventure. While there are essentially two specific categories of riders, within the group, you have different demographics and other distinguishable characteristics.

For example, you have the Harley-Davidson owners, a segment that makes up about half of our clients. This group is usually a bit older (35 and above). Lots of baby boomers got into riding Harley's, and they are passionate about the experience of riding together as a community. Most Harley riders tend to be event-oriented, often attending numerous events together. They celebrate their riding culture, often dressing the part and wearing leathers. This group enjoys the freedom and camaraderie that comes with riding. People from all walks of life are part of this community: doctors, lawyers, engineers, and blue-collar workers. Riding is an equalizer. When you get on the bike and you're in your gear, it doesn't matter what you do or who you are; it's the shared love of riding that's important.

Within the community, there's also the Metric crowd, which includes European imports such as BMW and Ducati. These riders tend to come from higher socioeconomic (mostly white-collar) backgrounds. This group is typically focused more on the engineering and mechanics of the bike rather than the culture. For the most part, they don't have as many organized bike events and are more into motorcycle racing and performance. They are big into events like MotoGP, MotoAmerica, and Superbike races. For them, it's about performance, engineering, and the quality of the bike. They love riding on roads with tight twists and turns, through canyons and other challenging features.

European riders on sport or touring bikes tend to be very safety conscious. For them, it's about being conscientious of the risks and mitigating those risks through proper riding techniques and gear. This group also tends to take classes to learn how to become a better rider or racer on the track.

Another segment is the Asian Metric market, which includes Honda, Suzuki, Yamaha, and Kawasaki. While the clients our member firms represent have street versions of these bikes, these manufacturers also make dirt bikes. Japanese street bikes tend to attract more price-conscientious buyers because the European options are usually more expensive. The bikes in this category tend to be more affordable and appeal to individuals who are looking for an alternative that is still reliable and highly functional at the same time. There is a lot more value in Japanese bikes, many of which are considered midlevel and are less expensive than both the Harley and European equivalents. Riders who select these bikes are typically younger and focused on racing, performance, and speed. Other riders in this segment use their bikes as a means of economical transportation or for a fun weekend ride to blow off some steam.

There are a number of rider categories within the motorcycle community. Furthermore, these differentiating factors vary based on demographics and lifestyle. Regardless, the overarching similarity of all riders is that they all want to have a good time, experience the road, and have a sense of freedom. Riders who pass each other on the street give each other a thumbs-up or a nod. They share something that other people don't. Motorcycle riders have a common bond, and they embrace this culture.

The motorcycle community has cultivated a positive culture of camaraderie that extends beyond the road. Not only do they create meaningful relationships with fellow riders, but they are also some of the kindest and most charitable people I know. Riders will donate time and money to help others in need — fellow riders and nonriders alike. They're very giving and resourceful, and they always lend each other a helping hand. If someone's broken down or parked on the side of the road, many riders will pull over and make sure they're okay.

In fact, our field-marketing team throughout the country is constantly assisting riders who have a dead battery, mechanical issues, a flat tire, or run out of gas. Each team member's van contains equipment — including spare fuel, portable air and jump equipment, motorcycle tools, and space — to transport a broken-down motorcycle.

In just the last few weeks, two of our field team members assisted stranded riders. One gentleman in Alabama had broken down on the side of the road on a rainy day, and Chris Litteral, our local Marketing

Manager, loaded his bike into the Law Tigers van and took him to the repair shop.

In Oregon, Todd Quinn, another Law Tigers team member, drove three hours to the coast and three hours back to help out a stranded rider and transport his broken-down motorcycle. Todd had received a Facebook message asking for assistance, and he responded by acting the same day without question or hesitation. Our community helps their own, and we all embrace and practice this within our program.

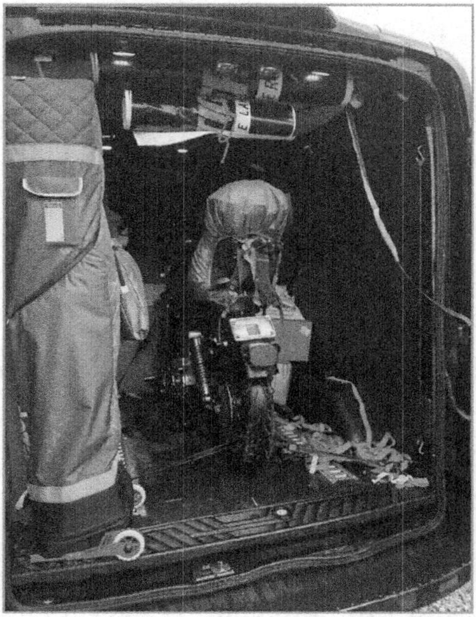

Helping a stranded motorcyclist

The Law Tigers program targets all aspects of the community within our model. We utilize the following taglines, "We watch over our own" and "We got your back" to convey that we're a part of this vast community, and we're here to help.

Even if you haven't been in an accident, we want to assist riders in any way we can. Whether it's getting you back on your motorcycle or helping you overcome some sort of adversity, we are a dedicated resource for educating riders, motorcycle industry staff, and clubs on safety measures, proper gear, and adequate insurance coverage.

Each market also has a budget that supports charitable efforts. We continuously give back to the community, not only in money and time, but through education. We want to show the community that we care, and one of the ways we demonstrate that care is by investing in them.

Staying involved is one of the most significant ways we interface with the riding community. Racing is one of many ways we connect with riders. We sponsor and partner with race promoters who host racing events. We support national, regional, and local races and race series throughout the country, including the American Flat Track series, EnduroCross, Arenacross, Supercross, and Steve Nace Racing, to name a few. Between the tickets we give away to our dealership partners, clients, and the public and the marketing support we provide by leveraging our grassroots, traditional, and digital resources, the association and support we provide is acknowledged and appreciated throughout the riding community.

We also sponsor and promote countless local and national bike weeks, dealership events, charity rides, poker runs, toy runs, bike nights, club events, and thousands of other motorcycle events throughout the country. Having a significant presence in almost 50 markets within 32 states — along with a network of

7,500 motorcycle shops and dealerships with whom we work, thousands of events we attend each year, and hundreds of clubs/organizations we support — affords us countless opportunities to engage with riders continuously.

At the core, it's all about community. There are so many facets of it that people participate in because it's a lifestyle. The Law Tigers brand truly represents who we are and what we do. When we market our program, we're not touting ourselves as ambulance chasers, but promoting the industry, the people, and the culture we all love and are a part of. To put it simply, we operate as a resource to members of the riding community.

Chapter

8

State of the Industry

One of the ways we remain innovators in this business is by keeping track of current industry trends. Some of the aspects we always consider are the state of the industry and changes taking place in the automotive space. As with any industry, it evolves and is in a constant state of change.

Overall, the motorcycle industry remains very profitable yet cyclical. There are shifts in new bike sales. While used sales may be up, new unit sales may be slightly down or flat, depending on the brand. Because these trends are cyclical, they are impacted by various factors, such as the economy and demographics.

Appealing to millennials is one of the ways that the industry is trying to increase sales. By developing more affordable bikes and new initiatives, the industry is making efforts to get millennials interested in riding. Another aspect that the industry needs to examine is changes that occur over time. Just because a millennial is not interested in riding when they are young doesn't mean they won't be interested when they're older and have the income to invest in a new motorcycle.

In terms of motorcycle trends, engineering and design are at their most innovative state. Manufacturers have taken steps to improve safety and enhance performance. One example is the implementation of anti-lock brakes that perform and handle better. New gear is available for riders to support bike safety, including lightweight materials such as carbon fiber, metals, and polymers used in helmets, boots, pants, and jackets. Several companies have even created jackets with inflatable technology that would offer increased protection to a rider if they were ejected from a bike.

The best way to prevent accidents is to educate riders and the public, so we focus our educational efforts on promoting safety. On the automotive side, the trends show that cars are becoming much safer than they once were. They are equipped with airbags and accident avoidance software and are engineered with safer structures designed to absorb impact and decrease injuries.

Because cars have become much safer, those in the automotive personal injury practice space will see less and less business over the next 10-20 years. Unlike motorcycle cases, automotive cases tend to be lower in value because the injuries, medical care, and associated costs with insurance are usually lower. Law firms need to generate more cases to make up that difference. (An average lawyer's fee in an automotive case can be $3,000 to $7,000 — much lower than in a motorcycle case.)

If a firm is spending millions on marketing, which large advertising firms do, it would need a substantial increase in the volume of cases to make up the difference. A considerable amount of legal and support staff would also be required to handle all of these cases, significantly adding to overhead. For those firms that are smaller in size with limited advertising budgets or those that aren't accustomed to spending much on marketing and advertising, trying to compete in the automotive or general personal injury space is extremely difficult. More competition — along with increased demand and advertising costs for television, outdoor, and online presence — makes it virtually impossible to break into an already saturated market comprised of a few well-funded, established firms that receive a majority of these cases.

On the other hand, with a motorcycle practice, your average fee can range from \$20,000-\$50,000 and can be handled with fewer staff, reduced operational expenses, little competition, and significantly lower advertising costs. While you'd spend some budget on traditional and digital marketing, a large portion of your cases will come from grassroots efforts and referrals, which are much less expensive from a lead/case acquisition standpoint. If you were to become a Law Tigers member, our nationally established brand, turnkey marketing program, and vast experience that drives thousands of motorcycle cases to our member firms would allow you to achieve your goals more quickly and efficiently than if you were to do it in an alternative fashion.

Overall, the trends in the automotive space are going to diminish case availability and reduce average attorney fees. Additionally, now that ride-sharing has become commonplace, fewer people own vehicles, further limiting opportunities for automotive personal injury lawyers. Conversely, motorcycles involve more risk, and riders' injuries tend to be more severe. An attorney's motorcycle clients may be out of work for extended periods, sometimes even permanently. They may even be disabled and need surgeries and medical treatment that could cost hundreds of thousands of dollars.

In these instances, injured riders will need an experienced attorney to help them get back on their feet. They're expecting you to assist them in obtaining compensation for their injuries. From an economic standpoint, the lawyer has an opportunity to drive value and a large-scale claim against the rider's insurance company and/or the other party's insurance. With motorcycle cases, the fees tend to be higher due to the injuries sustained. Generally, the insurance companies determine the payout amount based on injuries sustained, necessary treatment and care, lost wages, and pain and suffering.

To compare, let's say that there has been a car accident, and the client sustained soft-tissue injuries. She then goes to a physical therapist and other health care providers and incurs $10,000 in medical expenses. The insurance company may tender the policy limit and pay $15,000-$25,000, depending on coverage levels. In this scenario, the attorney's fee would be between $5,000 and $8,300. Even if there is additional insurance coverage, the value of the case and the resulting attorney's fee would be limited as a result of the injuries and medical expenses.

On the other hand, let's assume you have a client who's been in a motorcycle accident. Often, they've been hospitalized, and if they've sustained severe injuries, they will often experience months of medical treatment, loss of wages, and pain and suffering. In a case like this, the accident has significantly impacted their well-being and quality of life. In this scenario, if there's a reasonable amount of insurance, the case could be worth hundreds of thousands of dollars, if not millions. The resulting attorney fee would be much higher compared to a typical automotive case. Because of these facts, a motorcycle personal injury practice tends to be more efficient and cost-effective to handle, resulting in a higher return on investment. Without having to deal with a large number of clients — or support staff, for that matter — lawyers and their teams can take better care of their clients. The result is quality rather than quantity.

By focusing on the motorcycle community, the firm does not have to manage the needs of countless clients and compromise on service. With this value-over-volume approach, you don't have to deal with the challenges that come with a high-volume, lower-case-value practice. These challenges include staff management and related expenses, quality control issues, cash flow, and many other headaches associated with overhead and human resources. With a motorcycle practice, you can focus on managing your clients and your firm in a way that is client focused rather than operations focused.

Often, firms with large automotive practices are looking to turn cases and generate fees as quickly as possible. This is necessary to sustain astronomical marketing and advertising budgets as well as covering monthly operational overhead. This approach can compromise the outcome for both the client and the firm. By working with clients in the motorcycle community, attorneys and their teams are generally more fulfilled as this is a rewarding practice area for a host of reasons. All of our members tell me that our program allows them to really make a difference and change people's lives for the better. The riders appreciate that Law Tigers attorneys go the extra mile and feel as if they have a friend and advocate they can trust.

As I've said, Law Tigers strives to foster a relationship that is relational rather than transactional. While a number of our lawyers and legal staff are riders and they understand their clients' needs, those who are not can sympathize with what they are going through. During this process, Law Tigers lawyers help clients with their property damage claim, which is often very important to riders as they have an emotional connection to their motorcycle and gear. Law Tigers attorneys ensure that the insurance company understands the value of an injured rider's gear and leathers so they can be replaced. Ultimately, we want to ensure the clients are provided with ample compensation to replace and restore what they have lost as much as possible.

Our member law firms place a great deal of emphasis on getting clients healthy. As part of our network, members have access to a system of health care providers and other partners whose mission is to help riders recover physically, mentally, and financially. It's incredible to see riders with severe injuries and lost limbs get back on their bikes to ride another day. While they may have to make adaptions or get a three-wheeler to accommodate their injuries, we help them get there.

Riders are a different clientele, and working with them requires a unique approach. As compared to other types of clients, riders need more support and engagement. Our policy specifies that our member firms communicate with their clients at least once a month, though it's often even more frequent. It's simply a way to build and sustain a trusting relationship between the firm and its clients.

Even if there's nothing to report, we encourage our members to reach out to clients. For many, this is the worst time in their lives. Riders who have experienced a severe injury have a long, difficult road to recovery. Rather than simply being their lawyer, you and your team must be supportive and give them hope for the future. Counseling injured riders and making sure they have enough support to get through this trying time is the right thing to do and will pay huge dividends in the long run. This approach illustrates one of the main reasons we want to work with firms with similar values. A firm must be passionate about who it serves and able to put its rider clients' interests first if they want to work with us.

By choosing to represent riders, firms can utilize a sustainable model where the trends aren't going against them. Additionally, with the Law Tigers program, you have a well-known, reputable national brand behind you. Not only does this provide you with a pipeline of cases, but once the brand matures in your area and you continue to market, the cases will continue to come in for years to come, delivering constant cash flow. Our program offers so many layers of support that it allows our member firms to provide the highest level of legal representation to injured riders — while the marketing team delivers a continuous source of clients in need.

Chapter 9

Inside Law Tigers

Law Tigers is successful due to the work and efforts of our law firm members and the entire Law Tigers team, which makes up a specialized team of professionals. Each role is vital to our success, and each of our team members contributes unique skills that allow us to continue to grow and succeed. I have asked a cross section of individuals to share their experiences and their role with Law Tigers.

These talented individuals include AAMIL's Vice President of Field Operations (Lyonel Gammon); two team members from my father's Law Tigers firm, each playing a unique role in the organization (Bob Moellman and Scott Sirota); the Founder and Executive Director of the Arizona Motorcycle Safety and Awareness Foundation (Mick Degn); and two long-term Law Tigers attorney members (Tom Metier and Tim Kelly), each of whom owns one or more territories.

Lyonel Gammon

(Vice President of Field Operations)

Last year, I was promoted to oversee the entire 36-person field-marketing team under the role of Vice President of Field Operations for Law Tigers. Professionally, my background is in broadcast journalism. I worked in the radio industry for several years as on-air talent and did promotional work and sales. Essentially, my responsibilities included every aspect of the broadcast world for several years, and because I had always wanted to be a broadcaster, it was a dream for me. While I had envisioned myself becoming the guy on the evening news telling you what's happening in the world, after I had the opportunity to learn more about the field, I decided that it wasn't really for me.

I've always had an interest in marketing, advertising, and trying to grow a brand and a business. I also wanted to be the face and the voice that can help people or companies and provide an excellent service. When I made that transition out of the broadcast world 10 years ago, I came across the Law Tigers at an event that they participated in. Then, I found out they were looking to expand and open a new office in the Salt Lake market. Because I live in northern Utah, I thought, *Wow, this might be a great fit and a great opportunity*. After that, I decided to throw my hat in the arena, and fortunately, I was given the opportunity to become a local Marketing Manager for the brand. I started all of the preparations and the launch of the Law Tigers program here in the Salt Lake market. From there on out, everything was built on that.

With that opportunity, I was entrusted with a lot of freedom to bring ideas to the table and prove myself. I was always looking for ways to elevate the brand, provide a fresh perspective, and open up new opportunities. As things continued to go well, I eventually transitioned into my current role as the first official

Law Tigers Regional Marketing Director. Once I transitioned into that position, I was able to develop some new programs, initiate improved systems, training, and processes, and facilitate updated hiring practices to onboard qualified Marketing Managers and help launch new markets.

For the next three years, I oversaw our field operation for an increasing number of markets until we reached just over a dozen. As we continued to grow, we realized that we needed more help with launching and managing additional markets. Over the past few years, with the doubling and then tripling of new markets throughout the country, we added two more Regional Marketing Directors and are currently hiring two more. With this rapid growth, there was a need to add another level of management and leadership, and I was promoted to Vice President of Field Operations. I currently oversee 36 field-marketing staff, and this figure will likely reach 45-55 by the end of the year.

While some of the membership areas include a group of counties within a state, most markets usually make up an entire state. Each defined market has local marketing staff who visit motorcycle shops, attend motorcycle events, and meet with local motorcycle clubs and organizations.

The Directors oversee a specified set of markets and Marketing Managers within a region, and I supervise the Directors and run all large, national events. My goal is to be a resource for all team members and the community. I want to educate and teach my team how they can also be a resource for the community. Ultimately, our efforts will result in goodwill, motorcycle cases, and fees for our partner law firms, and we can keep improving on processes to grow their market share and revenue. The main objective is to meet all the goals that we've set for ourselves.

By implementing our marketing strategies, we can find opportunities to increase brand visibility while getting involved at the local level. We approach local business owners and offer them the opportunity to create a partnership. While providing support, we build a relationship within the community. Even if we're not an official sponsor of an event, you will see us. We take pride in aggressively getting our brand out there and becoming a resource. Not only do we support the motorcycle community, but we also help out local businesses in our selected markets.

For example, I have a friend who I advertise with at the Sturgis Motorcycle Rally. A few years ago, I went to South Dakota and helped him work his cattle. I happened to be in town, and since I have an agricultural background, I decided to help him out. While I work with him professionally, we have fostered and nurtured a strong friendship that extends past the advertising. With Law Tigers, we practice what we preach. We care about who we work with and who we partner with, and our actions show that. It's not just a 9-to-5 job for us. We live and breathe this brand. It's not just a job; it's who we are, and it's what we do.

I want people to know that regardless of the situation, the Law Tigers are here to help you out. Whether you've been involved in a motorcycle accident or need help tagging and branding your cattle this year, we're here. Where it's applicable, we want to be there for you.

Our Marketing Managers travel throughout their territories in branded promotional vehicles, fully stocked with promotional items, event equipment, and useful items needed to assist a fellow broken-down rider. Many of them encounter situations where their help is desperately needed. On numerous occasions, they've pulled over and loaded a broken-down motorcycle into their work van to assist a rider on the side of the road. Other times, they've either driven many miles to help a rider in need or pulled over to provide a stranded rider with fuel, a jump, a tire patch, or tools. It's not just words; for us, it's a true passion and way of life. As motorcycle riders, we're wired differently. We care for one another, regardless of what you're riding or who you are. Whether you ride as a group or you ride by yourself, it doesn't matter.

What matters to a fellow motorcycle rider is the passion, the desire, and the feeling of riding their motorcycle. We know why you ride. We care why you ride. At the end of the day, we're going to do all we can to make sure you can continue to ride. If something does happen, know that you've got a rider who cares about you, without even knowing you — someone who is going to go the extra mile to take care of you.

Law Tigers is built on the foundation of generosity. Our utmost goal is to be a fully integrated resource within the motorcycle community. We are not bottom-line focused; we are directly focused on the needs of riders and how to serve them best. My favorite aspect of working with Law Tigers is the ability to use my creativity. There's so much opportunity to pitch ideas to grow and evolve the program and invest back into the motorcycle community.

Bob Moellman

(Levenbaum Trachtenberg's Arizona Marketing Manager)

I am currently a Marketing Manager for Law Tigers, as well as a longtime rider. Presently, I'm the longest-running Law Tigers Marketing Manager, having joined them in 2007. Professionally, I have a background in marketing that made it easy to transfer over to several different industries. Initially, my territory was all of Arizona, but it was later split into two regions, and I now cover the west side of Arizona, north and south of Highway 51.

I spend the majority of my time visiting motorcycle shops and building relationships with the owners and the staff, making them aware of our services and what we stand for. I enjoy developing these relationships. My main priority is not to sell them anything, but to reach out and make connections.

Another important initiative of the Law Tigers program has to do with rider education, and I take part in these efforts quite often. I work with different charities regularly as well. The motorcycle shops I visit are frequently involved with personal causes, and we like to help support them.

To promote the mission of Law Tigers, I ensure alignment with our beliefs and values. Like most of the Law Tigers Marketing Managers, I always carry a set of jumper cables and spare fuel. If I come across a stranded rider, I help them get back on the road and to safety. It's a large part of what we do. I also help match riders with people who can repair their bikes. If a rider is ever in a motorcycle accident, they know we'll be by their side as Law Tigers to help them every step of the way.

Scott Sirota

(Levenbaum Trachtenberg's Law Firm
Practice Manager for Arizona, New Mexico, Utah,
and Southern California)

Early on, as a Practice Manager at Law Tigers, I had interactions with all of our clients. As we have grown, I now typically handle cases that involve our catastrophically injured clients. One story that stands out to me happened about 10 years ago. I met a mother and a father at a local hospital. Their son had been involved in a terrible motorcycle accident. He had come from Texas and had been attending Motorcycle Mechanics Institute in Arizona.

This rider wasn't wearing a helmet (Arizona is a non-helmet state), and he ended up getting into an accident with life-threatening injuries. One of the first people on the scene was a minister who comforted the injured rider, reassuring him that he would be fine until the ambulance arrived. He left his calling card with the rider and departed the scene. Later, in the hospital, the young man told his parents that he wouldn't have made it through without the kindness of that minister.

The parents wanted to visit the minister to tell him how much he had meant to their son and let him how much of a difference he had made to their son's recovery. They couldn't find the church and got lost, so they stopped at another church to ask for directions. Upon entering, they encountered a woman at the front desk, and they inquired about the minister. She asked them what their business was; they explained it was personal, and they just wanted to talk to the minister.

The woman then told them the minister died eight years prior and that the church they had been looking for hadn't been active in over a decade.

Sometimes you hear a story like this, and you don't think anything of it. I even brushed it off — until I saw the accident report from the first responders, indicating that a minister had been assisting our client. There have been so many stories involving our clients that are unique and inspirational. Being a part of that is truly rewarding.

Building relationships with our clients is a priority. We are with them every step of the way — which brings me to another story that involves a young client of ours in California. He had a tough upbringing and ended up dropping out of high school to take care of his younger siblings. Unfortunately, he had a horrific accident and lost function in his dominant arm, which eventually led to amputation. Because of the lack of support in his life, I sort of ended up adopting him in a way and saw him often. During his recovery, his child was born, and I even attended the christening.

With such severe injuries, we must represent our clients from the very beginning. A lot of the recovery takes place over many months, and it's essential to make sure we stay true to our word and support them throughout the entire process. Our job is to ensure that each client gets compensation for their injuries. I genuinely love what I do, and working for Law Tigers allows me to help fellow riders in their time of need.

Mick Degn

(Executive Director, AMSAF)

I currently serve as the Executive Director of the Arizona Motorcycle Safety and Awareness Foundation, a nonprofit organization founded in 2011 that works to reduce motorcycle accidents and fatalities. Initially, Warren Levenbaum helped to establish the organization and became a board member. Several years ago, Ari Levenbaum, Warren's son, joined the organization and currently serves as chairman. In the past eight years, we have raised over $1 million to support the motorcycle community directly. Our efforts are focused on getting individuals to take part in motorcycle training. New riders have access to programs that help them learn how to ride and to other training resources.

In Arizona, a number of motorcycle riders do not have a motorcycle endorsement. While some have no interest in receiving one, others simply cannot afford to go to a motorcycle class. We want to help riders have access to these classes and give them the opportunity to receive their endorsement. We offer a variety of scholarships that help motorcyclists within the community.

Our primary goal as a nonprofit is to engage with the community. As a result, we work closely with a variety of entities, including the police, state and federal governments, the National Highway Traffic Safety Administration, the Arizona Governor's Office of Highway Safety, the Arizona Department of Transportation's highway department, the health care community, and companies like Law Tigers.

We establish a partnership with each of these different entities. Not only are they supportive in our scholarship efforts, but we also receive grants from a variety of sources. These partnerships help prevent motorcycle accidents and educate the community on the importance of "sharing the road." In most cases, these accidents involve another vehicle. We want to emphasize the importance of looking out for one another and being aware of the other drivers and riders on the road.

Law Tigers has been able to support motorcycle riders by offering a variety of resources and services. Since our inception, Law Tigers has donated over $100,000 to our organization. They have also provided hundreds of hours of their time and energy by participating in our charity events, fundraisers, and motorcycle safety and awareness initiatives. Through their vast community network and numerous advertising resources, Law Tigers has also provided us with free billboards, television ads, vending space, and social media promotions to support our public initiatives. The cumulative value of these resources is easily in the several hundred-thousand-dollar range, which, as a nonprofit, we could never afford otherwise. At AMSAF, we believe that it is essential to partner with organizations like Law Tigers that are focused on helping individuals within the motorcycle community. Together with Law Tigers, AMSAF has been able to increase our education efforts regarding safety for riders, reduce motorcycle injuries and fatalities, and help save lives.

Law Tigers Member Attorneys

In addition to our AAMIL team and other partners, our network of lawyers plays a tremendous role in the success of the Law Tigers organization. Our members all share the common goal of serving and protecting the riding community. Whether that's through preventing motorcycle accidents or promoting motorcycle safety, a Law Tigers motorcycle attorney will be there for you. Not only do our member attorneys utilize the Law Tigers program successfully, but they live the lifestyle. Some are riders themselves, while others have partners or team members who ride. I have asked two law firm owners to share their experiences on being part of the Law Tigers program. As you'll see, they're as passionate and committed as I am, both to Law Tigers and the riding community!

Tom Metier

(Law Tigers Member Attorney: Colorado, Wyoming, Nebraska, Oregon, Washington)

Motorcycles have been a part of my life for as long as I can remember. After I graduated from college, I bought a bike and rode around the country.

During one of my trips, I was involved in an accident. It was late October, so it was chilly. As I was riding down the highway, there was a car at a stop sign. It pulled out right in front of me. My bike T-boned the car and my helmet hit the doorframe between the front and back doors on the passenger side of the vehicle.

Suddenly, there I was, lying on my back in the street in a strange place. I didn't know anybody, and I needed to be taken care of. I felt so helpless. My motorcycle was all banged up and I had severe pain in my knee. I'm taken to the medical clinic, and as I'm lying there, all I could think was: *What's going to happen to my motorcycle? How am I going to pay for my medical bills?* As I got up from the gurney, I discovered that I could walk pretty well even though my knee was messed up.

Without thinking clearly, I left the clinic and started walking. The clinic was about 2 miles outside of town, so I hitchhiked in and ended up at the police station. I saw the officer who had been on the scene and asked him if he'd gotten statements from witnesses. He said I didn't have to worry about it, but I panicked because I wasn't aware of the protocols. I knew that I wasn't at fault, but I was unsure of what would come next. Sensing my panic, the officer laughed and said, "Well now, son, just don't worry about it. Since you're worried about your motorcycle, let me take you to it."

We drove out of town a little way, and he dropped me off at a small motorcycle shop that looked really nice. Inside was a great big guy — probably about 6 feet, 4 inches tall and weighing about 250 pounds, with tattoos, a full beard, and a big smile. As I looked around, I saw beautifully restored motorcycles.

The owner asks, "You must be the guy who was riding the Triumph, a Trident 750?" When I say yes, he says, "Well now, you're going to love what I do with this bike. I'm going to take care of it." He wants to know where I live, and I tell him Northwest Iowa. He says, "Well, on Christmas Eve day, at about 5 a.m., you're going to get a knock on your door. Be ready because I'll be dropping off your motorcycle on my way to take my family out to Colorado for Christmas."

I felt so relieved that somebody was taking care of me and taking care of my bike. I hitchhiked back home. Sure enough, on December 24 at about 5 a.m., there's a heavy knock on the door. Outside, my motorcycle is on the back of a trailer. We rolled it off into a little garage lean-to I had out there, and he took off. I knew then and there that the kindness of somebody who follows through on their word, does what they're supposed to do, and takes care of an injured rider's bike is invaluable.

I went on to law school and left with a passion for helping people who have been physically or mentally injured in accidents. Based on my own experience, I had a particular interest in helping injured motorcyclists. By the time I came across Law Tigers, I'd already been practicing personal injury law in Colorado and Wyoming for many years. I was nationally known for doing brain and spine injury work, as well as teaching. It was during this time that I saw an ad for Law Tigers in Trial Magazine.

A couple of weeks later, at a trial lawyers convention in Colorado, I run into Warren Levenbaum. He's staffing a table and handing out Law Tigers brochures. I approach him and say, "Let's fold this thing up, go in the next room, and get this taken care of." At that point, he was looking for somebody to become a member of the American Association of Motorcycle Injury Lawyers, and I immediately knew that this was something I needed for my law firm and me. Our first meeting took place in early 2007.

By June of that year, we were open for business as the Colorado and Wyoming member of AAMIL, Law Tigers. We immediately started taking in cases. My practice was now devoted to representing seriously injured people. On top of that, we were able to begin representing much larger numbers of motorcycle riders, and we already had a pretty good-sized motorcycle injury practice to start. Because motorcycle injuries can be severe and involve a lot of brain and spine injuries, for us to be able to help more riders felt like home.

Motorcycle riders have always been especially important to me. It's not just a matter of transportation but a way that people contribute to their communities. Motorcycle riders do great things. They go on poker rides, work for children's hospitals, and so much more. Being able to contribute to that community is an honor for all the Law Tigers members. There are so many opportunities to give back. For example, we're there for the Christmas ride, delivering presents to children, and we also continue to work with children's hospitals. It's a great opportunity when you can help other people who, in turn, help even more people.

Through Law Tigers and the Metier Law Firm, we're able to leverage the opportunity for every rider and every member of the Law Tigers community. I take great pride in the fact that we can even make some financial contributions in addition to devoting our time. Through these contributions, we can make a big difference in the lives of a lot of people. Helping others is why we use the Law Tigers program. Currently, we have Law Tigers operations in Colorado, Wyoming, Nebraska, Washington state, and Oregon. It's been such a privilege. Combined with the other practices we do, it's a wonderful way to live for a lawyer, particularly a trial lawyer.

Through Law Tigers, our firm sponsors a variety of charity events. One of my favorite charities is Realities for Children, based out of Fort Collins, Colorado. Realities for Children has become a national model for charities across the country. They help kids who have been displaced from their homes because of parental violence, drug use, or other unfortunate situations. The organization takes these kids and helps them get through school, supporting them in their foster care situations and giving them college scholarships. They have the support of district attorneys, the foster home programs, members of the riding community, and other contributing members of the community.

They've built a tremendous facility here in South Fort Collins where families can go and meet with each other. It's an amazing thing. One of the events is the world's largest poker run. It took place on Memorial Day about four years ago and currently holds the record. Now they are going to recertify it here and try to expand it even further. Every Memorial Day and every Labor Day, there are big poker runs that attract thousands of riders. Through our firm and the Law Tigers program, we're a major sponsor of that event.

There's nothing like watching and listening to a child speak at a dinner for 500 people (all past or present contributors) and hear about how their life has been changed — how they now have the opportunity to get an education at a two- or four-year college. Motorcycle riders have the chance to be a part of a weekend adventure with friends and family, along with the chance to contribute to a worthy cause. They can help these children at Christmastime by donating and refurbishing bicycles and volunteering to help with their programs. Every little bit helps, and we're able to gather a lot of little bits to make it a great big thing. Law Tigers is central to that.

There are different types of poker runs that typically take place on a Saturday or Sunday. Most often, you organize a motorcycle ride that stops at four or five locations along the way. When you make your donation, you get a poker hand. At each stop, there's usually food, drinks, or even live music. At the end of the ride and once you've completed the circuit, they announce the winning poker hand. The winner gets a portion of the money that was donated, and the remainder goes to a chosen charity. Often, these events are organized by a motorcycle shop or other charities such as Realities for Children.

The values of Law Tigers not only extend to the community as a whole but also goes right back into the motorcycle community. It's a privilege to be a member of a national association of lawyers dedicated to taking care of riders and a program that provides security for motorcyclists throughout the country. Riders know that if they do get injured while riding a motorcycle, there's somebody there for them, no matter where they live.

There is no greater honor than meeting a family whose loved one has been injured in a motorcycle accident. We're able to work with them over time and get their family back to the place they should've been in had their loved one never been hurt. We go through some pretty tough things with hurt riders, and they have considerable fear about their future. To be able to help them through the legal process and the healing process is so gratifying.

People have asked me why I work so hard, and I always tell them, "I've never been to work, so I wouldn't know." After I started practicing law, I have had the honor of getting up and helping somebody every day. While I get paid for it, it's not just a job, but a privilege. Law Tigers has allowed my firm to grow and become even more successful. When I signed on with Law Tigers, my firm expanded to handle all of the cases. So far, it's been a gratifying experience for us to be able to help more people.

The Law Tigers method of marketing is highly effective. It allows the lawyers, their paralegals, and their staff to focus on what they do best — helping people. Not only are we helping injured people, but we also are helping their communities. To further aid the riding community, we support all of the rider training programs. Whether they're at motorcycle shops or independent safety programs, we even support state-sponsored programs. Through our rider education efforts, we educate them about better riding techniques, covering topics such as safety protocols when riding as a group. We also review how to understand traffic behavior.

It isn't just a matter of your handling your motorcycle; it also comes down to understanding what other drivers can and cannot see. We also look into what other drivers are likely to do — because they fail to look out for motorcycles. We teach riders how to conduct themselves around 18-wheelers, which is different from navigating other traffic. Because of the limitations on what the driver of an 18-wheeler can see, we educate riders on what they can do to avoid accidents and potential injury.

Law Tigers has developed systems and marketing programs that make every component of the program effective and profitable for the law firm. This, in turn, allows firms to help even more people. It's a win-win situation. One of the things I really like about Law Tigers is that I'm able to use a brand name in addition to the Metier Law Firm brand, effectively helping us segment our marketing. We're known for brain and spine injury, oil field injuries, and all sorts of high-end, unusual, and complicated cases.

However, with our Law Tigers practice, we're also well known for the specific practice of motorcycle injury. The Law Tigers name gives us a clear identity. Not only does Law Tigers provide riders with a golden opportunity to be safe, but it also allows them to participate in their community in a way that's positive and fulfilling. The same goes for lawyers who are interested in joining the Law Tigers family. Not only will you have the chance to become part of a group of expert motorcycle lawyers, but you'll have the opportunity to become a better lawyer, help more people, and experience limitless growth and success.

Tim Kelly

(Law Tigers Member Attorney: Chicagoland)

Ever since I was a young child, I wanted to be a lawyer because my dad was one. During my entire academic career, I was focused on becoming an attorney, which I did. I completed my undergraduate degree at St. John's University in Minnesota and went on to the University of Minnesota Law School. In 1972, I graduated from law school, passed the Indiana bar exam, and began practicing at my father's firm, Beckman, Kelly, Singleton, Levy, and Chris. In 1989, I decided it was time to open my own shop and established Kelly Law Offices, and I've been practicing there ever since.

When I started my firm, a lot of our business was insurance defense work. I decided I wanted to switch sides and become a plaintiff's attorney and represent injured people. This change led me to Law Tigers. Because I had been involved both as a defense attorney and a plaintiff's attorney in some motorcycle injury cases, I realized that those injuries were always serious.

I wanted to get more involved with motorcycle injury cases. At the time, Warren was handling the marketing for Law Tigers, and he sent postcards to plaintiff attorneys — that's how I found out about Law Tigers. Once I received one of the postcards, I began looking into the program.

As I developed my personal injury practice, I looked into ways to include motorcycle riders within our approach. I gathered information and investigated the available Law Tigers markets, and my firm then took on the Chicago market. Currently, half of our caseload is motorcycle accidents. In 2006, we made riders the focus of our personal injury practice. While we still take on other types of cases, our marketing efforts are focused on the motorcycle community.

I started riding as a young man. My father knew how dangerous motorcycles were and forbade me to ride one. Though I couldn't get one myself, I had a good friend who had two small motorcycles, and he would let me ride on the back of his. I started getting acquainted with bikes and began to ride on my own. As I got older, I got out of riding and eventually became a private pilot. I even had my own plane for about 15 years.

When I got into Law Tigers, I bought a bike, got my motorcycle endorsement, and started riding again. Once we started using the program, our phone was continuously ringing. We had never experienced such a high volume, and it's been such an enormous benefit to our firm. Because of how the brand works, our firm association now has automatic national recognition. For me, one of the main draws of the program was the legacy aspect. I knew I'd be passing my firm on to younger attorneys, and since it wasn't branded to me, but Law Tigers, our reputation would withstand, whether or not I was personally present at the firm.

The Law Tigers model fosters a genuine and authentic approach to their target audience — motorcycle riders. Not only do we relate to our clients, but we interact with them on a personal level. One case that stands out to me took place about four years ago. We received a call at our office from the father of a rider who was in the hospital. His son was in an induced coma as a result of a terrible motorcycle accident. A school bus had turned left directly in front of him.

This kid was so seriously injured that the initial responders did not think he was alive when they arrived on the scene. Although he sustained horrific injuries, he survived. When his dad called, he said, "They gave me my son's wallet when I came in. As I was going through it, I saw the Law Tigers card. I felt that my son had it there for a reason."

This card led him to us. That biker benefit card is one of the original Law Tigers marketing pieces. Without it, that father would have never reached out to us to work on behalf of his family. This is just one of the countless stories that I can share on how Law Tigers has been there for injured motorcycle riders.

Chapter

10

The Future of Law Tigers

Currently, there are 42 Law Tigers markets throughout the United States, each of which is operated by one of our carefully selected member law firms. At this time, there are an additional three markets with deposits placed on them. While we plan to expand into Canada, Europe, New Zealand, and Australia, we are focused on selling the remaining 24 U.S. markets over the next two years. These markets are considered exclusive territories.

In simple terms, we sell either the whole state or a portion of the state to one firm. Because there are only so many accidents within a state, we don't want to break up the markets to the point where there's not enough business for a lawyer to achieve a reasonable market share. In some of the larger states with higher injury/fatality figures, such as New York, Tennessee, Pennsylvania, Arizona, Ohio, Illinois, North Carolina, California, Texas, and Florida, there are multiple exclusive territories. The three largest states include Texas with four areas, Florida with five, and California with seven.

With plans to sell more markets to new and existing members, ultimately, we should then have over 50 Law Tigers markets up and running by the end of this year. If the trend continues and new and existing members continue to buy multiple territories, we will easily meet our target and focus our efforts on international opportunities, as I mentioned earlier. Ultimately, our goal is to become the worldwide, premier motorcycle injury brand that riders turn to when in need. When people are injured on their motorcycle, whether in America, Australia, New Zealand, Canada, or Europe, they will be able to get the very best legal representation available, regardless of where they live or where the accident occurred.

While Law Tigers is a successful program, there are extremely high standards and requirements that firms must meet to become part of our family. We aren't for everyone, and between the financial conditions, the background check, and the other standards that must be met, only the best firms are considered. We have a brand to protect, as well as the interests of our existing member firms and their clients. As riders, my father and I only want the very best firms representing fellow riders and the Law Tigers program. We want firms that are willing to litigate when necessary, and we don't want members who will compromise with clients legally or financially, for that matter. If we have a market available in your territory, we'll be happy to consider you. Please be aware that we are extremely protective of the brand, our members, and the riding public.

Conclusion

It has been an incredible 20-year journey, and the best is yet to come! When my father started the American Association of Motorcycle Injury Lawyers, he understood the power of marketing and branding. He felt that if you worked hard, provided a quality service, took care of people, and went above and beyond the call of duty, the riding community would rally behind us.

My dad also understood the power and benefit of developing a national association of like-minded law firms who could work together, learn from and support one another, and, ultimately, provide the highest level of legal service to injured motorcycle accident victims. He knew there were law firms similar to his throughout the country that needed to diversify and differentiate their message and services. I am fortunate enough to have been given the opportunity to help realize his dream and continue to build upon it to this day. Moreover, I am equally proud and honored to have been able to work by his side to make Law Tigers the preeminent national motorcycle personal injury brand that he envisioned.

While we have accomplished a great deal, there is still work to do. There are some remaining opportunities available in certain states and territories for qualified firms that want to become part of the Law Tigers. For those of you with practices in Canada, Europe, Australia, New Zealand, and any other country where you think our program may benefit you and the riding community, please let me know.

Thank you for taking the time to learn about the Law Tigers program. If you read this book, there was obviously some reason for doing so. Regardless of your motivation, I hope that you took something away from it that can help you with your practice. While I feel as if I covered the essential principles, practices, and operational structure of Law Tigers, a book only goes so far. If you see value in what I shared and you would like to know in more detail how our program functions and how you might benefit, please don't hesitate to reach out.

We are always searching for like-minded firms that are passionate about taking their personal injury practice to the next level to partner with us. If you are looking to grow your practice in a meaningful way with a turnkey marketing program that delivers a substantial number of motorcycle cases, now is the time to consider becoming a Law Tigers member. Find out if a Law Tigers territory is open in your state by visiting us at

membership.lawtigers.com

Once you've arrived at **membership.lawtigers.com**, the easiest way to get started is to complete our online form, and we will be in touch with you to set up an exploratory meeting to share with you more about our industry-leading, niche motorcycle practice.

Visit **membership.lawtigers.com** today to join Law Tigers — America's Motorcycle Lawyers! Don't forget to download our FREE niche marketing guide written especially for personal injury lawyers.

About the Author

Ari Levenbaum is co-owner and COO for the American Association of Motorcycle Injury Lawyers, also known as the Law Tigers. He started working part-time for AAMIL in 2002 while maintaining a full-time middle school science teaching position for several years. In 2006, he left an eight-year teaching career and transitioned into a full-time role with AAMIL — first as a Marketing Manager and later as the Vice President of Marketing. In 2014, he purchased a minority ownership interest in AAMIL, and in 2016, he acquired an additional share to make him an equal partner with Warren Levenbaum, his father.

Law Tigers is a professional association of Motorcycle Injury Lawyers. Ari oversees all operations, marketing, branding, and public relations campaigns and initiatives. Formed in 2001, the American Association of Motorcycle Injury Lawyers, or Law Tigers, provides superior personal injury legal services to the motorcycle riding community.

Ari has cultivated and maintained multilevel partnerships with industry representatives and their constituents, including motorcycle clubs, vendors, manufacturers, and dealerships. He is responsible for developing a highly effective integrated marketing system, with the objective of brand awareness and trust among a diverse community of motorcycle riders and industry-related business owners. As a rider, Ari has a unique understanding of the motorcycle riding industry and community, proving tremendously beneficial in his role with the Law Tigers.

Ari is married to Kathleen Levenbaum, his wife of six years, and has a 23-year-old stepdaughter, Ashley. He has spent almost his entire life in Arizona, where he attended Chaparral High School and the University of Arizona, earning a Bachelor of Science in Political Science. Later, he was awarded a master's degree in Educational Administration from Northern Arizona University.

He and his family currently reside in Arcadia, a Phoenix suburb. Ari and his wife enjoy biking, walking, hiking, and riding their electric scooters around the neighborhood. He enjoys taking his Can-Am UTV and Ford Raptor off road to the desert around Phoenix and on forest trails surrounding his log cabin just outside of Flagstaff. Ari is also an avid motorcyclist, both on and off road, and he enjoys riding anything with a motor. His current collection includes several Harley-Davidson street bikes, a Kawasaki Ninja, and a couple of dirt bikes.

Made in the USA
Monee, IL
04 November 2026

67387212R00089